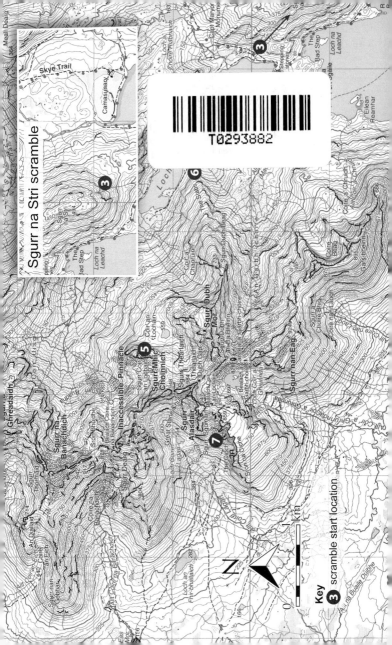

Sgurr na Stri scramble

Skye Trail

Camasunary

The Bad Step

Loch na Leachd

Sgurr na Stri

Key

3 scramble start location

About the Author

Adrian is a mountain guide and photographer living on Skye. He has been climbing since the 1980s with a CV that includes Alpine north faces, big walls in Yosemite and first ascents on the White Cliffs of Dover.

After a BA in history from King's College London, Adrian devoted himself to climbing and photography. Jobs were often temporary and a means to finance climbing trips. His work in the outdoor industry included 12 years at Ogwen Cottage in Snowdonia, one of the few places in the UK to regularly take secondary school students multi-pitch climbing.

Adrian and his wife, Bridgette, live at the foot of the Cuillin and feel they are living their dream life. Together, they run a guiding and photography company, All Things Cuillin, and have set up the very popular Facebook group of the same name.

Skye's Cuillin Ridge Traverse

Strategies, advice, detailed topo booklet and 10 classic scrambles

by Adrian Trendall

CICERONE

Juniper House, Murley Moss,
Oxenholme Road, Kendal, Cumbria LA9 7RL
www.cicerone.co.uk

© Adrian Trendall 2020
First edition 2020
ISBN: 978 1 78631 043 9

Printed in China on responsibly sourced paper on behalf of Latitude Press Ltd
A catalogue record for this book is available from the British Library.
All photographs are by the author unless otherwise stated.

Maps are reproduced with
permission from HARVEY Maps,
www.harveymaps.co.uk

Updates to this guide

While every effort is made by our authors to ensure the accuracy of guidebooks as they go to print, changes can occur during the lifetime of an edition. Any updates that we know of for this guide will be on the Cicerone website (www.cicerone.co.uk/1043/updates), so please check before planning your trip. We also advise that you check information about such things as transport, accommodation and shops locally. Even rights of way can be altered over time. We are always grateful for information about any discrepancies between a guidebook and the facts on the ground, sent by email to updates@cicerone.co.uk or by post to Cicerone, Juniper House, Murley Moss, Oxenholme Road, Kendal, Cumbria, LA9 7RL, United Kingdom.

Register your book: To sign up to receive free updates, special offers and GPX files where available, register your book at www.cicerone.co.uk.

Front cover: Perfect weather for the Bad Step on Am Basteir

Contents

View to Cuillin Ridge
from summit
of Clach Glas
(Classic
scramble 9)

Symbols used on maps and topos

∼	route
∼	alternative route
S	start point
F	finish point
>	route direction
①①	numbered waymark (main route)
①①	numbered waymark (alt route)
✿	numbered waymark (hidden from view)
A	abseil
B	bivi site
W	water
ER →	escape route

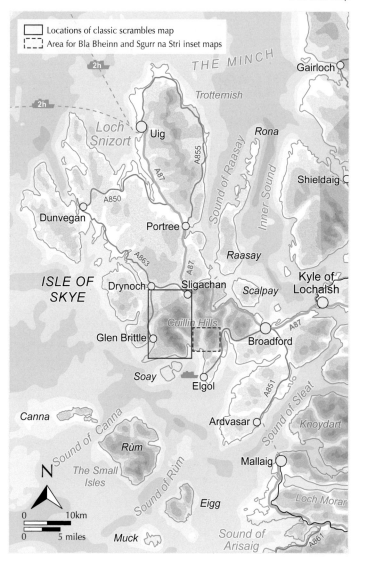

Locations of classic scrambles map

Area for Bla Bheinn and Sgurr na Stri inset maps

THE MINCH

Gairloch

2h

2h

Trotternish

Loch
Snizort

Uig

Rona

A855

A87

Sound of Raasay

Shieldaig

Inner Sound

Dunvegan

A850

Portree

A863

A87

Raasay

Kyle of
Lochalsh

ISLE OF
SKYE

Drynoch

Sligachan

Scalpay

A87

Cuillin Hills

Glen Brittle

Broadford

Soay

Elgol

A851

Canna

Ardvasar

Sound of Sleat

Knoydart

Sound of Canna

Rùm

Mallaig

N

The Small
Isles

Loch Morar

0   10km
0   5 miles

Eigg

Sound of Rùm

Muck

Sound of
Arisaig

A861

Descending from Sgurr nan Eag towards Caisteal a' Garbh-choire. Easier lines exist on scree to the left (Section 1)

Introduction

The very special brand of ridge scrambling found here can have few equals in the whole world.

Gordon Stainforth, author of 'The Cuillin'

Skye's Cuillin Ridge has been described as 'the holy grail of British scrambling' (British Mountaineering Council) and 'the jewel in the crown of Scottish mountaineering' (Jamie Andrew – a climber, motivational speaker and quadruple amputee).

A well-known climbing venue since the late 1890s, people soon began to wonder if a traverse of the ridge was possible in a single outing. It wasn't until 10 June 1911 that Leslie Shadbolt and Alastair McLaren completed the first traverse of the Cuillin Ridge – and they did it in a day. Their time of 12 hours and 18 minutes from first to last summit is a time that many modern teams would be only too pleased with. Previously it had been thought impossible, that it would be 'a feat of the gods' and take perhaps three days or even longer.

Shadbolt referred to the traverse as 'a great day' and later recalled that 'we thought we might try the traverse of all the peaks, an expedition about which there had been a good deal of speculation'. Those first traversers were well ahead of their day with the route not being repeated until 1920. The route taken has become known as The Great Traverse and over the years the record has fallen to a remarkable 2 hours 59 minutes and 22 seconds. This speedy traverse was set by Finlay Wild, a runner and climber of repute.

If you are reading this, then the Cuillin Ridge probably needs no introduction but the statistics below flesh out the nature of the beast.

Traversing the ridge can be a delectable experience as much of it is on the cusp between climbing and walking thus allowing for fast, exhilarating

Section	Distance and ascent	Terrain	Time
Approach	7km and 900m of ascent	Rough walking	3 hours
Ridge	12km and 3000m of ascent	Scrambling to grade 3, technical climbing to Severe and 3 abseils or down climbs	10–15 hours
Walk out	6km and 900m of descent	300m of scrambling and rough walking	3 hours

Climbers ascending to N Top of Bidein (Section 8)

progress unimpeded by ropes or pitching. Much of the ridge is tinged with an air of seriousness where a slip could prove fatal, and the height gain alone puts it in the league of the North Face of the Eiger. But when you throw in the set piece technical climbs – such as the Inaccessible Pinnacle (In Pinn) and the Thearlaich Dubh Gap (T-D Gap) – several abseils and yet more scrambling, it adds up to a magical journey in sensational situations. The technical climbing grades might alarm walkers but shouldn't set off too many alarms for competent climbers.

It is no coincidence that the Cuillin Ridge is the first route in Ken Wilson's uber tick-list, coffee table book, *Classic Rock*. A ridge of 900m mountains rising straight out of the vibrant Hebridean seas, it has attracted climbers and walkers for generations. The 11 Munros, miles of knife-edge scrambling and

iconic climbs help explain its attraction as does the obvious linear nature of the challenge and the continuously interesting, high-quality scrambling and climbing.

Although a huge challenge, it is achievable by many climbers and here lies much of its appeal. The climbing may be long but it is never too hard or sustained. With preparation and practice, a helping of luck, a good level of fitness and the right mental attitude, the ridge is within the grasp of many climbers. For many, it is a dream route but with a little effort (well, quite a lot, actually) it is one that can become a reality. Although Alpine-like in length and quality, the ridge is surprisingly accessible and as such not too committing with many variations, bypasses and escape routes back to civilisation. Indeed, ease of escape helps to explain the high failure rate since it is all too easy to throw in the towel at the first sign of difficulty and be back in the pub in a few hours.

For many climbers, traversing the ridge may well be their one and only visit to Skye but many return again and again to delve into the complexities of the ridge. The 'Tolkienesque' landscape with sharp ridges and towering cliffs, mist shrouded peaks and extinct volcanos is unique. Some people strike lucky and succeed in their first attempt but, for the majority, it requires the conjunction of the right partner, good weather, physical fitness and mental strength to produce a winning formula. Cuillin experts reckon that perhaps only 10% of climbers succeed on their first attempt.

The Cuillin Ridge seems to be a never-ending source of interest. In 2019, if you typed 'Cuillin Ridge' into Google, you'd get 93,000 results; and if you searched UK Climbing's forums, you'd find more than 350 separate threads on the subject as people try to find answers to their questions about logistics, rope length and gear lists. Despite such a wealth of available information, until now there hasn't been a single universal source of information about the ridge. This guide collates the author's years of experience and information from numerous different sources in order to help bring the challenge of traversing the ridge within reach of many climbers, scramblers and walkers.

Shadbolt wrote an account for the Scottish Mountaineering Club Journal entitled *The Cuillin Main Ridge* and stated that 'in common with... most people who have climbed in the Cuillins (sic), I have always looked with

A classy descent of Pinnacle Ridge to top a perfect ridge in a day

longing eyes at the great stretch of narrow ridge and speculated on the possibility of making a continuous climb along it from end to end in one day'. Not everyone can, or will want to do it in one day, but, like Shadbolt, you 'can endeavour to translate the dreams of the winter fireside into the realms of accomplished action'.

Preparation and training

Being well prepared is a key ingredient of a successful traverse. Good planning and preparation will increase your chances exponentially.

Partner

Partner selection is crucial and any incompatibility will only be exacerbated during the stress and strain of a traverse. Not only will you spend a very long day, or two, together but the pair of you should train together as a team, so compatibility is a prerequisite. Choose a partner with similar levels of fitness, determination and stamina to yourself – but don't overlook things like shared interests and a similar sense of humour. An ability to get along well with each other is the second most important thing after safety.

Pick your partner with care, rather than coercing a reluctant boyfriend or girlfriend, for example. Remember your life can, quite literally, be on the line with your choice of partner.

Play to each other's strengths, so if one of you is a much better climber then that person should lead all the technical rock pitches. Finishing the ridge is more important than being able to list the traverse as alternate leads in a logbook. Be prepared to help each other out and don't be too proud

Enjoying the relatively easy route across Collie's Ledge (Section 4)

to accept help. For example, if one of you is flagging, then the other can offer to carry both rope and rack.

Ability is not the be all and end all – climbers operating right at the limit of their ability have completed the ridge, having stacked the odds in their favour by researching the route and training hard etc. Conversely, top climbers have failed due to underestimating the undertaking.

Physical fitness

A high level of fitness alone won't guarantee success but it will improve your odds and enable you to make the most of any weather window.

Walking, cycling and running are all good for general fitness. Going to a wall or climbing hard outside won't necessarily help but the more grades that you have in hand, the better prepared you will be to effortlessly solo the easier parts of the ridge and cruise the technical pitches.

There is no substitute for sport-specific training so long scrambles and lower grade climbs, long, rough walks and the like will be brilliant practice. Consider link-ups of long easy climbs – choices abound in North Wales and the Lake District.

All training is best done carrying what you anticipate using on Skye. Thus, a fully loaded pack and your choice of footwear should be obligatory. Wear approach shoes and a pack when training at your local wall and concentrate on grades appropriate to the Cuillin. Getting the miles in is more important than flashing hard routes.

Make sure you train whatever the weather. Movement on damp or wet rock, navigation in poor visibility and setting up a bivi in the dark should all reap dividends in getting you ridge fit and ensuring these things become second nature. Think outside of the box and maximise what you have to hand. Your walk to work can be built into the training; wear a rucksack and balance along kerbstones or have a quick traverse of a stone wall. Or, walk up flights of stairs in your office rather than taking the lift. Sea defences and bouldery beaches provide good training opportunities.

Psychological fitness

Most teams will not only be physically exhausted by (or long before) the end of the ridge but also mentally drained. Lots of people after their first attempt on the ridge comment on the scale of the exposure – not just the steep cliffs and big drops involved but the continuous, unrelenting need to remain 100% switched on as you concentrate on the terrain. Mental resilience and a determination to continue is essential, especially on the second half of the ridge which can seem never-ending. You cannot simply plod on and push through regardless because you must stay alert and concentrate on every foot and handhold. Don't make the mistake of underestimating the mental pressure of constant scrambling in potentially dangerous situations for hour upon hour, especially as the time ticks by and the darkness draws ever closer.

With clean cut holds, The Spur on Sgurr an Fheadain is doable in the wet (Classic scramble 2)

Become slick

Part of the US Navy SEALs' mantra is 'slow is smooth, smooth is fast', and this is what you need to aim towards. Your movement along the ridge needs to be smooth, an uninterrupted flow forwards. Haste has no place and will lead to mistakes and premature expenditure of energy. Practice pacing yourself and make every single action efficient. Learn from mistakes on your practice days out.

Here are a few hints on being slick:

- Have food and drink to hand in order to negate the need to stop and remove your pack then reverse the process. Keep food in your pockets, water in a bladder and a drinking tube carefully positioned so as to be accessible.
- Refine your clothing system so there is zero faffing with layers on/off/on. If conditions dictate then wear a hat and gloves then remove and put in pockets and vice versa.
- Start with the rack arranged and clipped to the leader's harness ready for the off. Put the rope in a stuff sac or stuffed in pack ready to deploy so as to reduce time wasted uncoiling it and the risk of tangles. Only use the rope when absolutely necessary. Nothing is going to consume time more than endless pitching or abseiling on terrain that can be scrambled up or down-climbed. The weaker climber can use a screwgate to clip into a figure of eight on a bight for speed and after any use of the rope the leader can just take in more coils once the knot has been freed from the screwgate.

- Have a map and guidebook in your pocket and readily accessible rather than in your pack. Map cases are a real faff and will definitely be a big no-no for climbing/scrambling.
- Get into the habit of saving energy. For example, contour everything from the big hills to the smallest rock traverse. Losing/gaining height is bad and requires an unnecessary expenditure of energy. Adopt the motorway mindset of maybe going a little further than if you were driving on A roads but the process is quicker and more efficient. Constantly scan slightly ahead and planning each foot placement and hand hold.
- Communicate with your partner and stay within sight of each other so the second doesn't have to make the same mistakes as the leader. Point out the easiest line to each other, warn about loose rocks and generally help and look after each other, especially as the day progresses and people tire.
- Get into the habit of overly loosening your pack straps as you remove them so they are easy to put back on later.
- Pack your rucksack so that anything needed during the day is easily accessible. Bivi and cooking gear can go at the bottom of your pack with items needed during the day close to the top.
- Wear clothing appropriate for the conditions and don't hesitate to shed layers to avoid overheating. Remember, if you can't be bothered then you probably should.

- Concentrate all the time both for safety and navigation. It's all too easy to be distracted while talking and to lose track of where you are especially in poor visibility.
- Make any transitions from walking/ scrambling/climbing slick and avoid unnecessary time wasting.
- Ensure your shoe laces are well done up and if they are overly long, cut them down. Lots of modern foot-wear comes with laces that seem to come untied incredibly easy, so experiment. Stop and remove stones from your footwear as soon as you notice their presence rather than plodding on and getting blisters.

Remember, practice makes perfect.

Research

Research is probably the most com-mon denominator between successful teams. Make sure you read accounts, watch videos on Youtube, look at pho-tos and peruse guidebooks until you know the ridge inside out. Become a Cuillin bore, a Cuillin obsessive and ruthlessly devour all available informa-tion. Below are some recommended resources:

UK Climbing has several informative articles and a very active forum with more than 350 different threads on the Cuillin alone (www.ukclimbing.com).

YouTube has lots of videos rang-ing from amateurish, nausea-inducing head cam productions to full scale advertorials. The pick of the latter include a traverse sponsored by Salewa and another by Rab. In the former, a reporter from *Trail Magazine* is guided along the ridge over two days whilst the latter features running the ridge in a day.

There are several guidebooks and inspirational **books** about the Cuillin mountains. Details can be found in Appendix B.

Practice

Your preparation should involve long days that include rough walk-ing and scrambles or enchainments of easy climbs. Practice, for example, in Snowdonia, on Idwal Slabs then Cneifon Arete before carrying on along the tops to do something on Tryfan. For the full pre-Cuillin practice, you could then carry on to do the Snowdon Horseshoe or the Amphitheatre Buttress. If you are planning to do a multi-day ridge, then get out and prac-tice with full bivi gear and actually bivi out so that everything becomes second nature to you.

If time allows, try to get to Skye and get on some of the routes listed in the chapter in this book on classic scram-bles. Take care though not to use up any good weather on your practice and then find that when you come to do the traverse your luck has run out.

Make sure all your technical climb-ing skills are up to scratch and you can lead quickly with a pack, build belays quickly and abseil in a safe fashion. Practice leading with a fairly minimal rack so that you get used to placing less gear and running things out a bit more than usual.

Climber on slabs/corners leading up to Sgurr a' Mhadaidh's third top (Section 7)

On the summit of Gars-bheinn about to start a one-day traverse (Section 1)

For a team to succeed, it needs to solo the vast majority of the ridge. Time is lost each and every time the rope is used. What could be soloed in a few minutes might take an hour to pitch. Practice soloing on easy ground and gradually build up the difficulty. Remember, there is as much descent as ascent so practice down-climbing.

Try and allow a few extra days so you can get used to the Cuillin gabbro and basalt; how good the friction can be on the gabbro and how slippery damp basalt can be. Get out and train for the ridge but, if possible, recce some of it in preparation for the big day.

Planning

Take on board all the available information and plan according to your capabilities, the weather, available time and desired outcome. Decide on a one-day or multi-day traverse, and whether your approach will be from Elgol or Glen Brittle. Work out how you will retrieve cars from Glen Brittle or Elgol once the ridge is finished, as well as where you will be based on Skye (Glen Brittle, the Sligachan, Broadford or further afield).

Buy any specific hill foods before you get to Skye. Most people will travel through Fort William, which has a range of outdoor shops for last minute purchases, as well as gas for stoves etc. It also has large shops such as Lidl and Morrisons for the more budget conscious. Do you need to stash food/water etc high on the ridge? An Dorus, the notional midpoint, is easily accessed from the path by the Glen Brittle Youth Hostel. Pre-placing water makes good sense especially in hot conditions or for single day, light and fast attempts.

Preparation

Last minute plans and preparation are vital. Be ready for the weather window you have been hoping for and don't get out of sync with the weather patterns. It is no good if your gear is saturated from practice days in poor weather when a glorious forecast is posted and you will kick yourself if you are exhausted when the weather comes good.

A rest day prior to the traverse makes good sense. Sit on the campsite and chill, rest your legs and eat and drink to capacity. Peruse the guides and maps, pack and repack, go to the pub but don't overdo it. Make sure you have food and water ready for your return, which may be after the shops and pubs close. In your rush to get away, don't leave your tents or other accommodation in a mess because once you're off the hill, you will just want to crash out. Have everything packed and good to go so you simply need to wake up, dress in your pre-chosen clothes, breakfast and go. Don't forget to set an alarm (or two).

Strategy and tactics

The big, strategic question is what are you realistically hoping to achieve? A complete traverse with all the climbing bits, starting at Gars-bheinn and finishing on Sgurr nan Gillean? Or, will you be satisfied just getting from Gars-bheinn to Gillean, perhaps making the tactical decisions to omit the T-D Gap and Naismith's? In many ways just getting from end to end is a fine achievement even if some bits

Ascent to summit of Sgurr Thearlaich from top of The Great Stone Chute (Classic scramble 7)

The steep second abseil
from Bidein (Section 8)

have been bypassed. The whole ridge is slightly artificial since not even the most hardened purist will take the most direct line the whole way; it's just not possible. Remember that purity of the traverse comes a long way after safety and enjoyment, the two most important factors for a successful hill day. My partner on a traverse, Kevin Woods, brilliantly described our day as a 'full house – 11 Munros, four classic climbs and a bunch of other spiky bits for the hell of it'. We did the whole ridge, all the Munros, all the climbs and descended by Pinnacle Ridge for a perfect day. I have had good traverses when climbs have been missed out and bypassed taken due to the weather or other problems. I call this the "Cuillin Ridge Light"; a tactic which opens up the traverse as a possibility for many walkers and scramblers who are not hardcore climbers.

Direction of travel

The vast majority of summer traversers go south to north and there are good reasons for this but the north to south approach has its own benefits. South to north means you get some classic climbs, finish on the stunning summit of Sgurr nan Gillean and can descend to the Sligachan for a celebratory drink.

But south to north means some of the most complicated and sustained sections like the four tops of Sgurr a' Mhadaidh and Bidein come late in the traverse when bodies and minds are already fatigued. To face the Bhasteir Tooth so close to the end is a big challenge. It's a long initial slog out to the

start on Gars-bheinn and there are complicated descents if going south to north; Sgurr Thearlaich to Sgurr Mhic Choinnich, Banachdich to Sgurr Thormaid.

A north to south traverse means some of the harder, steeper climbs can be abseiled; the last part of Sgurr nan Gillean's west ridge; Am Basteir, Bhasteir Tooth etc; the second and third tops of Sgurr a' Mhadaidh; and the T-D Gap. Instead, there are tricky climbs up to An Caisteal and Bidein's main summit.

On balance, there are good arguments for either direction but to experience the best climbs and a better finish, south to north is arguably more popular for good reasons. There's also more chance of all the abseils having in situ anchors.

ONE DAY OR TWO?

Light and fast, or heavier packs but the amazing experience of a night high in the mountains – which would you prefer? If you are just there to tick the ridge and have the necessary ability and fitness, then a one-day traverse is a good option. Others will relish the longer time spent in the mountains. There is no right or wrong way.

TRIAD: The Ridge In A Day

This can be a gamble, putting all your eggs in one basket. If you are so exhausted that you do not finish, then it is unlikely you are going to physically, let alone mentally, recover enough for a second attempt on this trip. If the gamble pays off and everything is in alignment then the outcome will be brilliant.

It can be thrilling to move fast and light with minimal gear and be down in time for a celebratory drink. It's a great feeling to do the ridge in a day and, in some ways, it's the purest approach. Unless you are exceptionally fit, however, TRIAD will be a suffer fest.

To do it, cut things to a minimum and only set off if the forecast is perfect. In good weather, you could ditch spare clothes, perhaps just taking a lightweight waterproof. Take a minimal rack and short rope, safe in the knowledge that if things go wrong there are plenty of places to drop out down to the Glen Brittle road in a couple of hours. Going as light as this is a risk you must accept in order to manage the ridge in a day.

If the weather is going to be hot then consider pre placing water at An Dorus, or, better still, get someone else to carry it up.

TRIAD has the bonus of only requiring a small weather window to offer a chance of success. To succeed, you will need to solo everything except the technical climbs and abseils. If the forecast is good, then be prepared for queues at the T-D Gap as other people will have seen the forecast. Either leave very, very early so as to arrive at the gap before anyone else or, if you are confident of a speedy traverse then leave later so as to be behind the early starters and arrive to a crowd free gap. The only other blockage is likely to be the In Pinn. But if you are moving fast you can still get there before the munro baggers arrive mid to late morning.

Retrieving a cache of food/water at An Dorus (part of Classic scramble 4)

CREST: Cuillin Ridge Expedition Style Traverse

The multi-day (usually two-day) approach can be a satisfying way to do the ridge and spend an extended period of time up high. This is for mountain lovers rather than teams that just want the ridge tick. It's also great for keen photographers with the chance of a great sunset and sunrise. What better way is there to chill out after a long mountain day than eating and drinking endless brews while looking out to

Typical stone-walled bivi site. Note midge net being worn

Hebridean islands and the ridge traversed and that still to come?

There is less urgency with this approach, and no need for such an excruciatingly early start. Time should be less pressing so there is some leeway to cope with delays at notorious bottlenecks like the T-D Gap or In Pinn. Water is not as scarce as the naysayers would have you believe so you don't have to carry debilitating amounts.

If you do decide to bivi, then make sure it's going to be comfortable. An uncomfortable night may well ruin your chances of finishing the ridge. Make sure all your gear is up to the job and try to pick a comfortable site.

Remove any obvious rocks that will dig into you. If it's windy, then use one of the many stone shelters or consider descending on the lee side of the ridge a short distance. However, remember if there are midges about then a breeze is beneficial.

A good rest combined with rehydrating and a decent meal are the key for success on day two. Set up things as soon as possible, rehydrate and eat then relax. A good bivi will enhance the whole traverse.

The downsides include having to carry much heavier/bulkier packs, which reduce the enjoyment factor, as well as the need for a longer weather

BOTH CREST AND TRIAD ARE OPEN TO VARIOUS OPTIONS

Some teams walk into Gars-bheinn and bivi. The next day you can stash the bivi gear and move fast and light. This means you get to experience a high bivi, get the approach and 900m ascent out of the way and your legs have the night to recover. Arriving by the last boat from Elgol could make for an excellent evening. Slowly wander up Gars-bheinn, cook dinner and fill your water bottles as high as possible, then continue to the summit and start the ridge. Stop at one of the stone circles, brew up and rehydrate before enjoying the evening.

The major downside of the above is having to retrieve your gear. Ideally, friends or relatives would be coerced into getting your gear back. Potentially, support teams could meet you on the ridge at various places such as the In Pinn. or An Dorus with bivi gear, food, water and so on.

Your team could place bivi gear, food and water in certain places for you but this means you are absolutely committed to getting to where they are hidden. Also, it potentially wastes two days placing and retrieving the gear but it does make for nice light packs. If you pre-place gear then be certain that you can recognise the hiding place especially with the possibility that you may be arriving in the dark or in poor weather conditions. Remember to go back to remove any bottles or rubbish left in caches. Abandoned water bottles are becoming an increasing problem on the ridge.

On a tactical level, there are lots of choices that can be made on the hoof depending on how time, tiredness and the weather are doing. The **Cuillin Ridge Light** tactic would have you always taking the easiest option. Most (but not all) of these easier options are shown as green alternative routes in the Topo Booklet, enabling you to mix and match to suit your ability and experience:

- T-D Gap or bypass it and do Sgurr Alasdair's south-west ridge
- King's Chimney or Collie's Ledge
- An Stac or bypass it
- The In Pinn can be bypassed if queues make a long wait necessary
- Bidein can be bypassed on its northern flank
- Naismith's or Lota Corrie Route or bypass Am Basteir entirely to the north
- Descend from Sgurr nan Gillean by the W ridge, SE ridge or Pinnacle Ridge.

window and the greater chance that the forecasters may have got things wrong. A lot of people who opt for CREST could have managed TRIAD with its correspondingly much lighter loads. Much of the challenge of TRIAD is psychological.

Escape routes

If things are not going too well, there are plenty of escape routes. In fact, despite seeming remote, the Cuillin is very escapable and thus the commitment lower than one might expect for a route of its size. Section route maps in the Topo Booklet have escape routes marked on (ER).

Escape routes include:

- Bealach a' Garbh-choire
- Bealach Coir' an Lochan
- Bealach Mhic Coinnich
- Bealach Coire an Lagan
- South-west ridge of Sgurr Dearg
- Bealach Coire na Banachdich
- Western shoulder of Sgurr na Banachdich down to Coire an Eich
- Eag Dubh
- An Dorus
- Bealach na Glaic Moire
- Bealach Harta
- Down into Coir' a' Tairneilear via the gully below the An Caisteal abseil
- North-west ridge of Bruach na Frithe
- Bealach nan Lice
- Bealach a' Bhasteir

Bivi sites and water sources

There is much evidence of where people have spent nights high on the ridge and it is interesting to wonder what future archaeologists will make of the stone circles. Below are some of the ridge's bivi sites:

- Gars-bheinn and along the ridge to the north-west has various bivi sites.
- Sgurr Dubh an Da Bheinn and Bealach Coir' an Lochain have lots of bivi sites that are close to the spring about 100m below the T-D Gap and

easily identified by the vibrant green moss surrounding it.

- The top of the Great Stone Chute has been used for bivis.
- Sgurr Sgumain bivi cave is especially useful if conditions turn nasty.
- The north ridge of Sgurr Thearlaich has a couple of good sites with stunning views up to An Stac and the In Pinn.
- Sgurr Dearg has lots of flat areas and, if conditions turn bad, there is the In Pinn bivi cave.
- Bealach Coire na Banachdich is another good site due to the proximity of water at about 700m. The best bivi sites are south of the bealach with stone circles built.
- The col between Sgurr Thormaid and Sgurr a' Ghreadaidh has good bivi sites.
- On Sgurr a' Mhadaidh, there are several bivi sites just up from An Dorus. There is the possibility of descending for water on the Glen Brittle side but it is a fair descent.
- Bealach na Glaic Moire has stone circles, some grass and water usually not too far below, but you might need a mug or straw to access it.
- Bealach nan Lice has stone circles and a spring 100m below the bealach. It's visible from above due to the vibrant green moss surrounding it.

Some years there will be large snow patches on the ridge as late as the end of May – and these can be a real bonus. A straw or drinking tube of some kind is useful for getting to water partially hidden below rocks.

Deer enjoying the spring below the T-D Gap

A NOTE ON RUBBISH AND HILL ETIQUETTE

Always use your common sense when using the hills but due to increasing popularity, the Cuillin needs to be looked after for future generations.

Please take all rubbish away with you. If you carried a full water bottle or can up, then it's a no brainer to take the empties down. If you pre place bottles of water then please make sure you retrieve them. Tissues and toilet paper are increasingly being discarded high in the hills and are unsightly and a biohazard. Take them home. Do some research about going to the toilet in the hills but remember, the Cuillin is a high mountain environment with a fragile, easily disturbed ecosystem.

Please do not build cairns, scratch arrows and directions on rocks or cause any unnecessary erosion or damage.

Gear

The cardinal rule in terms of gear is that light is right but not at the expense of safety. Remember, every extra gram has to be carried every single step of the way. Huge rucksacks or packs festooned with gear strapped to the outside suggest inexperience and a mentality of covering every possible eventuality. Extra gear can transform a single day attempt into a nightmare of exhaustion as you struggle in the dwindling daylight. If you take emergency bivi gear, for example, you are more than likely to end up using it.

Pack everything in your rucksack before you travel to Skye. Make sure it all fits and you can climb without being too impeded by it. Get out and practice with all the gear you will be using. The Cuillin traverse is no place to be trying out new gear which may, or may not, be up to the job.

Packing

Pack everything you will be taking before you go so there are no unpleasant surprises with weight or bulk. Try meticulously to save weight. Avoid duplication of items in both team members' packs – for example, sunscreen, insect repellent, toothpaste, lighters, stoves etc. Keep things like your sleeping bag in a waterproof bag and avoid the fad of having lots of different little bags for every item. Neither sleeping nor bivi bags need to be in separate stuff sacs. Just bundle them into your rucksack and compress them with the rest of your gear. Consider using your bivi bag to put water sensitive items (like sleeping bags) in. Try to avoid anything that will be sticky or leak and make a mess. Make sure sunscreen and the like are in bombproof containers and only take a small amount rather than the large bottles they are sold in.

Rack

Some teams have such large racks of gear that locals often joke that some secret big wall has been discovered. A huge rack suggests you lack the confidence and/or skill to tackle the ridge. As the visionary alpinist Mark Twight said: 'The size of our rack represented a huge judgement against our ability and confidence'. There are only three short, set piece climbs and all can be bypassed if conditions or mental attitude are not right. None are harder than Severe.

A rack is a very personal thing so it needs to be selected according to

Climbers on NE Ridge of Sgurr Mhic Choinnich with views to An Stac, In Pinn and the ridge beyond

RECOMMENDED RACK

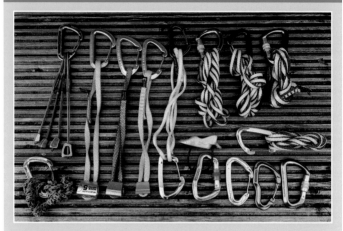

Typical smallish rack of gear for an experienced climber traversing the ridge

- Rocks on wire – sizes 3, 4, 6 , and possibly 8 , on a single wire gate karabiner
- Rockcentrics – sizes 3, 4, 5, each on a single wire gate karabiner
- 240cm sling x1 on a screwgate karabiner
- 120cm slings x3, each on each on a wiregate or screwgate karabiner
- 60cm sling x1 with two wiregates
- Wiregate karabiners x2
- Screwgate karabiner x1

experience and advice. Refer to the box for what I would take – others might want much more or soloists may dispense with it altogether.

Each person will need a screwgate and belay device and possibly prussik loops and a sling and screwgate. Consider taking a nut key to remove stubborn gear and some cord/tape to use for abseils; most abseils will have slings in place but you may opt to replace them and you also have the option of using the cord/tape should you get off route and need to retreat.

Gear that can double up is a bonus. Thus the Rockcentrics can be used for protection but also as short extenders and threads. Long slings can be shortened and used to extend runners, threaded round chockstones or placed on spikes.

Cams are heavy and not strictly necessary. Much of the climbing is very traditionally protected and climbs such as the In Pinn can be protected entirely with slings if you so choose. Long slings are better than short extenders which increase rope drag and also the risk of gear being lifted out.

Rope

The entire ridge can be done with a single 35m rope. A short rope means less weight and is much easier to manage both coiling and short roping. Many will take a longer rope and this does give you more options especially if things go wrong and you have to do longer than normal abseils. Taking a 35m rope rather than a 50cm or 60m rope is probably the easiest single way to save a lot of weight and bulk in your pack.

The rope needs to be thick enough to handle well for the short roping so super skinny ropes are not ideal and will soon get trashed on the super abrasive Cuillin rocks. Lots of guides use a 35m Beal Joker, which at 54g per metre is one of the lightest single ropes available. The Joker is ideal for the ridge but does require experience since it is very thin and may well be very slick in some belay devices.

Harness, helmet and head torches

All harnesses, helmets and head torches need to be as light as possible. There is no need for super comfy, padded harnesses with masses of gear loops. You won't be falling off (hopefully) and hanging around and you will only have a minimalist rack.

Comfort is important especially for walking in because you don't want to be continually taking the harness and off. Modern helmets are very comfortable and a good idea given the amount of loose rock and potentially other climbers knocking things down. If it's comfortable you will be happy to keep it on rather than just wear it for the climbs and then using it as extra ballast in your pack.

Make sure you can fit a head torch to the helmet and put it on before it is dark enough to need it. One set of batteries will easily last for a traverse so ditch any spares and set off with just a brand new set in the torch.

Pack

The type of pack you take is largely down to personal preference and depends on whether you are going for a one or multi-day traverse. Simple, light and robust are characteristics to look for. Simple designs will have no unnecessary features that add weight and can snag on things. Some people will take a small pack otherwise you are tempted to take too much but I nearly always use a rucksack of around 45 litres. Being a bit larger means it is easy to get gear in and out without a struggle. This saves time and frustration especially when trying to cram the rope or rack back inside after a climb. Compatibility with a water bladder is a useful feature and enables you to keep hydrated while on the move.

Choose your pack and footwear carefully and make sure you test your gear in conditions appropriate to the ridge (Sgurr a' Mhadaidh, Section 7)

Footwear

The old school of thought is that walking boots are de rigeur because they provide ankle support and more comfort on scree and the descents. If you are happy climbing to Severe with a pack on and have comfortable footwear then go for the boot option.

A whole industry has spun up manufacturing so called 'approach shoes', which combine the qualities of a trainer or fell running shoe with a climbing shoe. They are much better than boots for climbing in and have a much more precise fit and sticky rubber soles. The downsides are a lack of ankle support and generally not being waterproof. The latter shouldn't be too much of a problem since if it is raining then you will probably be abandoning the ridge. If you opt for approach shoes you need to be used to wearing them for such long hill days on very rough ground with a pack.

The rough Cuillin rock can play havoc with any footwear so consider smearing glue on the stitching to protect it from abrasion. It might not look pretty but it extends the life of the shoe considerably. With care, approach shoes can last longer than you might expect but with abuse they can be trashed on a single traverse. I have worn a pair of approach shoes for a six-week period in the Cuillin and they covered 240km with 27,000m of ascent. They were trashed by the end but had seen a huge amount of use.

If you are thinking about rock shoes to change into then perhaps you aren't ready yet for the ridge. Changing in and out of footwear is a waste of time and if you don't have the grade to spare to be able to rock climb in approach shoes or boots then you may well struggle to solo the scrambling, which is a prerequisite for success. Boot or shoe is a personal choice – whichever you opt for, make sure you train in them rather than arriving at Glen Brittle with virgin footwear. Go for a comfortable fit and bear in mind that your feet will swell over a 15-hour day.

Clothing

The type of clothing you need will depend on time of year, weather forecast and style of the traverse. A one-day traverse in perfect conditions might just require a light windproof and hat in addition to what you are wearing. For multi-day trips, think about the large temperature ranges that are possible and be prepared with warmer clothes for cold clear nights.

Socks should be comfortable, tried and tested. Merino wool mixed with manmade fibres work well (pure wool seems to wear out very quickly).

Trousers need to be hardwearing to survive the rough rock. Large pockets are useful for keeping hill food, route instructions and your map etc to hand. Shorts are not recommended due to the abrasiveness of the rock.

Underwear should preferably be of manmade fibres so as to dry quickly when you sweat.

Baselayer can be long-sleeved so as to keep arms warm and double as protection from the sun. Manmade fibres are best although some merino wool/manmade fibre mixes work well. 100% wool tends to get clammy and stay damp.

A **fleece** will provide a useful warm layer. A thin, hooded fleece with thumb loops is ideal and can be combined with a thin Pertex **windshell**.

A **duvet jacket** could be considered as an addition especially if you are going to bivi. Synthetic is best given the prevailing maritime climate.

Waterproofs will hopefully not be needed. You probably won't need a full metal jacket of heavy Goretex since if conditions are that bad you will be heading down. Lightweight waterproofs work well, are obviously light and pack down small.

Gloves provide useful protection against both the cold and the rough rock. A pair of thin liner gloves take very little space but may save the day if conditions change. Gloves are also useful for protection against the rough rock and rope handling especially if you

Leather gloves being worn on Bidein (Section 8)

31

aren't used to it. Big name climbing gear manufacturers make thin leather palmed gloves but they are expensive so a useful alternative can be either leather workmen's gloves or gardeners' gloves.

Headgear is invaluable for keeping you warm or cool so take a hat and something to protect you from the sun. Buffs are very versatile. Make sure your choice of headgear works well with your climbing helmet. You should consider taking sunglasses depending on the weather forecast but especially if it's going to be sunny and there is still snow around.

Bivi gear

Sleeping bag

Most people prefer synthetic bags due to the possibility of them getting wet. However, down bags are lighter, pack smaller and hopefully you will be setting out with a good forecast (and probably only for one night) so it won't be too disastrous should it get damp. Personally, I take a 1 season very light down bag and wear all my clothes in it happy to offset a slightly chilly night for a light pack over two days.

Bivi bag

I have only used Goretex bags and they work pretty well. I have seen people literally soaked with condensation when using bags made of other materials so Goretex is well worth the added cost. A zip top is preferable to the cheaper models with draw cords, which are harder to seal against the elements.

Remember, bags can tear easily on rough ground so choose your bivi carefully and consider putting your sleeping mat on the ground under it.

Sleeping mat

Lots of people take Thermarest-type mats but these are very vulnerable to the sharp rocks of the Cuillin so care is needed with choosing your bivi site. Consider a closed cell foam mat cut down to two-thirds of its full size, so just long enough to stretch from hips to shoulders; the rope can be uncoiled and used for padding under your legs and your rucksack as a pillow.

Stove

Gas is the way to go. It's clean, easy, quick and there are no worries about liquid fuel spills or leaks. Light is best but think about stability and wind resistance if going for the ultra-light models. Jetboil-type stoves are brilliant; not the lightest but completely self-contained with windshield, pot and cup etc all in one. Don't rely on built in-igniters – always take another lighter or windproof matches.

Cutlery etc

A spoon or spork should suffice since you won't be engaging in cordon bleu cooking. A largish cup can double as a bowl to eat from.

Water bottles

Consider taking extra bottles or a spare bladder so you can descend to a spring and take back plenty of water for the evening and next day.

Evening meal, breakfast and lightweight cooking gear

Food and drinks
Preferences will vary according to personal taste but whatever you take, make sure you have tried it in the hills prior to your ridge attempt.

Trail food to eat during the day
Trail food should be kept easily accessible so it can be eaten little and often, perhaps in trouser or fleece pockets or a pouch on your hipsack belt. Here are some ideas to consider:
- Fruit pastilles or jelly babies
- Fig rolls (although these can be too dry in heatwave conditions)
- Cereal bars (test them and opt for the more moist varieties)
- Energy gels in small sachets (particularly useful for one day traverses)

Liquid for the day should also be readily available so Camelback-type bladders are ideal and enable you to drink without stopping. Fill bladders and bottles etc and drink your fill as high as possible on the approach. Remember, lots of teams give up due to running out of water/dehydration. Hydration tablets not only replace lost salts and sugars but the pleasant taste can encourage you to drink more and stay hydrated.

Dinner
Boil-in-the-bag or dehydrated meals are very quick and easy to prepare, don't mess up the pans and the water can double for a hot drink. On the downside, they are expensive and boil-in-the-bag meals are heavy.

A cheap, easy and light alternative is a packet of cous cous, slices of salami and a cup-a-soup. Quality chocolate for pudding followed by copious hot drinks of your choice constitutes a fairly palatable meal. Keep water handy so you can rehydrate without getting out of your bag at night. A small bottle of whisky or a hip flask can enhance morale no end.

Breakfast

Again, quick and simple is the key with breakfast. Instant porridge only requires boiling water and can be made in a cup – consider adding cranberries or sultanas to it as well. Drink as much as is available. Breakfast bars are good but some can be a bit dry.

Miscellaneous

Depending on the time of year, consider taking a head net and/or some sort of repellent like Smidge to counter the midges. Remember, they don't fly if the wind is 4mph or more so exposed bivi sites on the ridge may be midge-free.

Besides midges, the other wildlife worry on the ridge is ticks, which may well latch onto you especially lower down on the walk in where deer are prevalent. Tick cards are worth their weight in gold to remove these stubborn blighters and are available from chemists.

Toiletries should be kept to a minimum – you shouldn't really carry more than a toothbrush and a small container with enough toothpaste for the team, toilet paper, sunscreen (if the weather's good) and lip salve.

Take a phone for emergency use and possibly to check the weather forecast on a multi-day traverse. Mobile phone reception is poor to non-existent in Glen Brittle, Elgol etc but pretty good when on the ridge itself. Check your

particular network has coverage before you set off. You might find a small camera useful to record events (or you could rely on your phone).

Make sure there is no duplication of unnecessary gear between partners. It may sound excessive but to save weight and bulk consider taking things out of individual stuff sacks and containers. Thus, there is no need to keep a bivi bag in a stuff sack. Unless there is a forecast of heavy rain, don't bother with a dry bag but use the bivi bag as a pack liner and bundle things inside it.

Navigation

Should you be lucky and have great weather with wall-to-wall visibility, you may well wonder what all the fuss is about. More likely, visibility will be less than ideal and you will immediately realise why people talk about the complexities of Cuillin navigation.

Navigational errors can rapidly eat into the daylight hours, are morale sapping and the lost time is hard to catch up. In fact, playing catch-up can often lead to a vicious circle of pressing on as fast as possible and making more errors. Abseil slings left on spikes, signs of wear ending in an impassable cliff, and dead end paths can all be indications of navigational errors made by previous teams. Conversely, signs of wear, abseil slings etc can and do mark the correct route so you need to be selective and use common sense. In theory, a ridge sounds easy to follow but in practice it is hard to envisage a more complex navigation scenario.

Descending slab/rib towards Sgurr a' Mhadaidh's third top (Section 7)

Maps

The best map by far is the Harvey's Superwalker XT25 Skye: The Cuillin. It is incredibly detailed and has a huge amount of information but even a map of this scale cannot show every minor detail, so use it with care. The map is double sided with 1:25,000 on one side and a close up of just the ridge at 1:12,500 on the other. Note that on the Harvey's map the contours are at 15m intervals with 75m index contours. Consider cutting the map to size so you just take the 1:12,500 ridge enlargement. Start out with the map folded to the relevant place and follow your progress continually.

Compasses

The Cuillin is notorious for its magnetic rocks and as such compasses cannot be relied upon and must be used with discretion; try holding the compass at shoulder height well away from the rock and move about a bit and see if the reading changes or not. Compasses are small and light and can provide useful information so long as you are aware of the possible limitations.

GPS

Like the compass, don't be over-reliant on a GPS, which may or may not be as accurate as its manufacturers would have us believe. The correction error of some smartphone Apps may mean your actual position is tens if not hundreds of metres out. In the Cuillin with its convoluted twists and turns and hazardous drops, an error of tens of metres could be catastrophic.

GPS accuracy can be variable. Where several features are close together, symbols may be displaced for clarity. Positional accuracy greater than 10m is not guaranteed (from the Harvey's map). Total reliance on technology is never a good thing because electronics can get wet and batteries can fail but a compass and GPS can be additional tools to more traditional navigation with a map and constant interpretation of the ground around you. A map works anywhere in the Cuillin – any mistakes are down to user error.

GPS units can come into their own in poor visibility and can often help make sense of the extremely complex geography of the ridge and your location on it. Your GPS should be able to provide you with a grid reference but it is well worth downloading as large a scale map as possible onto your GPS. The recommended Harvey's map can be purchased as an App and used with ViewRanger. Also with GPS, you can log recce routes or download routes from the internet.

You should definitely not just rely on a GPS unit as your sole means of navigation and consider taking spare batteries.

Mobile
Most people will take a mobile phone with them on the ridge to keep in touch, make phone calls, take photos and for use in case of an emergency. Phones can double up as a GPS and are a great back-up to both a standalone GPS and map but, again, be aware of their battery life and susceptibility to damage.

Knowledge is far more useful than any electronic device so do your homework. Read all the route descriptions available and match them to photos and maps so you are well prepared about what to expect. Prior knowledge is the best recipe for success so get out and recce the more complex areas. This can provide days out when the weather is not good enough for a traverse and when there is less pressure to be fast so you can move more slowly and really get to know the route. If you have a GPS with you then you could waymark various points for later use.

Climbing, scrambling and ropework
The ridge requires the full range of techniques from mountain walking on rough terrain to pitched rock climbing. To succeed, the speed/safety equation needs to be balanced. Soloing is obviously fast but with no margin for error. Pitching climbs is potentially very safe but also time-consuming so a balance needs to be struck whereby you are fast enough to finish the ridge but within acceptable (to you) safety margins. Most teams will use ropes for

E Ridge of In Pinn showing different styles; seconding on a rope and soloing (Section 5)

the climbs and abseils, the exceptions being speed merchants who will solo up and down everything.

Speed versus safety is the critical equation and one that is very much a matter of personal choice based on experience and conditions. Thus, some climbers will want the assurance and safety of a rope on a climb such as the In Pinn, yet others will be happy to solo it.

On a south-north traverse, there are only four set piece climbs and five abseils:

	Grade	Height/ length
Climbs		
T D Gap	Severe	20m
King's Chimney	Very Difficult	25m
In Pinn	Moderate	65m
Naismith's Route	Severe	40m
Abseils		
T-D Gap	-	10m
In Pinn	-	17m
Bidean 1	-	17m
Bidean 2	-	11m
An Caisteal	-	10m

That's only 150m of climbing and less than 70m of abseiling – very little out of 12km and 3000m of ascent and descent. The scrambling is a grey area between walking and climbing but it is the area where the traverse will be won or lost. Scrambling, possibly using a rope on harder sections, can be a good compromise between speed and safety and allow a lot of ground to be covered quickly but it definitely needs to be practiced. Hopefully your team will be a partnership of equals but if not then the more proficient climber may well end up doing a lot of short roping.

All rope work needs to be slick and efficient. Every time the rope is deployed, time is lost. A short rope, such as a 35m, involves less coiling, less rope to get tangled and is less weight than a more normal length of 50 or more metres. Consider just stuffing the rope in your pack with an end knotted to a strap so it is easily found and then it can be quickly pulled out with no faffing around, uncoiling or flaking the rope out to ensure no tangles. If one partner is significantly faster, they can carry the rope and rack which eases their colleague's load. The faster partner can make haste as a climbing pitch is approached, sort the rope out at the base of the climb and build a belay. Having tied on to the rope, they are ready to shoot off as soon as their belayer arrives.

To succeed on the traverse, you need to get into the mindset of climbers from days of yore when things were

Short roping on easy terrain as descent is made to Bidein (Section 7)

Guide and two clients on S ridge of Sgurr a' Ghreadaidh demonstrating the use of short roping and showing the serious nature of the terrain (Section 6)

of necessity simpler and as a result swifter. Protection was just a rope, the leader really did never fall and yet huge mountains were climbed, teams moved quickly and, percentage wise, there were probably very few disasters. The crucial things were that these climbers knew their limits and the limits of their minimalistic gear and operated within these parameters.

Technically, 'short roping' is a guiding technique with a guide safeguarding the less able/confident client. The guide will be operating well within their own personal comfort level, happy to not only effectively solo but certain they can protect their client. 'Moving together' refers to a pair of more or less equal climbers scrambling/climbing

simultaneously perhaps placing runners or weaving the rope between natural spikes etc.

Much confusion exists between definitions of short roping and moving together but more than likely you will be using a mix-and-match approach, selecting different techniques and seamlessly moving from one to the other. You need to be constantly assessing the terrain ahead and making judgement calls. Typically, on easier ground the leader might move forward keeping the rope tight on the second so that any slip is halted before it can develop into a fall with catastrophic results for both team members. As a steeper section is approached, the leader will drop the coils of rope so

CONSIDERATIONS FOR SHORT ROPING

- If used on too easy ground, it will slow things up and be frustrating for the second.

- If used on terrain that is too hard for the technique or your skill level then it can potentially very dangerous and could prove fatal to both members.

- Both team members' experience. Can you both cope with the technicality of the climbing? Can you both cope psychologically with the position, exposure etc?

- The nature of the terrain such as loose rock, scree or slippery rocks.

- External conditions such as changing weather like precipitation or strong winds.

- Does the nature of the route enable the leader to stay directly above the second so as to protect them and reduce the risk of a swing?

- Is a slip or fall likely, how serious would the consequences be and if there was a slip are you confident of halting it before it develops into a fall?

giving himself enough to climb the difficulty. The second will climb as the rope goes tight either as the leader continues to move up or as the leader belays quickly using a spike etc.

Short roping on serious terrain is extremely demanding for the leader who needs to be making a continuously updated dynamic risk assessment.

Here are a few handy hints:

- Make sure coils are over rucksack straps so they can be deployed easily.

- For speed, look for natural belays such as spikes and use them as direct belays. Once you start building anchors then things will really slow up. You need to be confident at anchor selection and be happy to use spikes and blocks directly.

- Consider wearing gloves so the rope can be more easily grasped and a slip stopped.

- It's all about judgement, constantly thinking ahead and making dynamic risk assessments.

- The leader needs to respond instantly to any slip by the second before the momentum converts a slip into a fall, which could be terminal for both parties.

- Recognise the demarcation between short roping/moving together/pitching and be ready to switch between them as the situation demands.

- The bottom line is that you must ensure what you are doing is safe and within safety parameters with which you are both happy.

- Remember, you cannot control the laws of physics and gravity no matter how much experience you have, so behave accordingly.
- Don't be constrained by the tightly laid down guidelines marketed as the must-be-used method. Be flexible and think outside the box.
- Ropes do not always need to be kept as taught as guitar strings; at times, this can be very disconcerting and counterproductive to the second who feels pressurised to move quickly and thus may make mistakes.
- Tie a figure of eight on a bight in the rope end and use a screwgate to clip on and off when the rope is needed. Over the course of a traverse this will save a lot of time tying and untying knots.

- Sometimes, for example on an awkward descent, it may be better for the 'guide' to go first, it being easier to demonstrate the moves rather than describe them, and then he can spot the second.
- Above all, only use the rope when absolutely necessary. It's only too easy for the second to become over-reliant on it and continue wanting to have the psychological aid of the rope even when it isn't strictly necessary.
- For short roping to be safe, the leader has to be as certain as they can be that they won't fall and, at the same time, be certain they can safeguard their second should they slip. If the make-up of your team suggests that much of the ridge is going to require short roping then

Climber high on second pitch of Naismith's Route (Severe, Section 10)

perhaps the disparity in ability and confidence between the two of you is too great to make a traverse viable.

- Short roping and moving together is really outside the scope of this book but there are numerous resources available in print and on the internet and many instructors run courses. Needless to say, these are not techniques to learn on the job as you traverse.

Grades

This guide covers the full range from walks through scrambles to relatively easy climbs. Grades given are for optimal conditions (ie dry, summer conditions). In damp, wet or wintry conditions, they will be much harder. The routes in this guide are all relatively remote and involve fairly long walk-ins so are more serious outings than roadside routes of similar grades.

Traditionally, scrambles are grade 1, 2 and 3. Once the scrambling gets harder than grade 3, it falls into the realm of climbing and gets a climbing grade.

Grade 1 should present few problems for reasonably fit, experienced hill walkers. Hands may be needed but holds will be large and obvious and the exposure should not be too great. Descent and/or retreat will be fairly easy.

Grade 2 will be more sustained and require more use of the hands and the exposure may be much greater. There may well be short, technically harder sections. Route finding and retreat will be harder.

Grade 3 is a level harder. Moves will not necessarily be obvious, the rock may be steep and exposure may well be great. Many hill walkers may well prefer the safety of a rope on this grade. There may be very exposed down-climbing on the route. Also, retreat may be difficult so the ability to abseil can be useful.

Moderate holds will normally be fairly obvious but some of the moves will be hard and often in very exposed positions.

Difficult holds will definitely need climbing skills as the route can be much more technical with difficult moves in exposed and serious positions. Gear placements to protect the climb may not be obvious.

Very difficult will require a reasonable level of climbing skill and technique. Holds may be small and the position very exposed.

Severe has increasing difficulties and more technical, less obvious climbing.

Weather

With its maritime climate, Skye gets a range of weather and the prevailing conditions may well make or break your traverse. In good, settled conditions you may get great views. Navigation can be relatively easy under such conditions, the rock dry and grippy, and the views stunning.

Things become tougher when the weather closes in and navigation can become problematic. Gabbro is grippy but wet rock is still no fun and you may end up pitching bits that many might normally solo up.

Wet, slippery rock as climber ascends slabs and corners on Sgurr a' Mhadaidh's third top (Section 7)

The weather will be one of the major factors in determining failure or success. Perhaps rather unfairly, Skye has a reputation for being absurdly wet but statistically it is drier than Fort William. When the weather comes from the north or east then any precipitation will have fallen on the mainland so Skye should get dry weather. Conversely, weather systems from the south and west will be wet, having come in from over the Atlantic. Fronts can travel fast and you need to be ready to act immediately should dry weather be forecast.

Make no mistake, progress is going to be slow to impossible in rainy weather. Bad weather has two major adverse effects, drastically reducing both visibility and friction. None of the rock will be pleasant but basalt when wet can be lethally slippery, especially slabs. Progress will slow to a crawl and only the very stubborn or stupid will continue. However, the ridge does dry rapidly and progress may well be possible in showery weather so long as the showers don't coincide with the technical climbing sections. Visibility will be seriously reduced in bad weather with the consequent navigational problems and reduced speed as maps are double checked and errors corrected. Prior knowledge is a big help in less than perfect visibility. Take note of the forecast height of the cloud base and work out if you will be in the clag or not.

Strangely enough, rip roaringly good weather can lead to as many failures as bad. Sunburn, dehydration, teams running out of water and general lethargy

High on An Stac Direct (Section 7)

can all result from wall to wall sunshine. High winds will obviously cause problems on exposed ridges so the southern Cuillin may well be more sheltered if winds are from the north.

Ideal conditions would be a forecast of dry weather with the summits clear but higher cloud filtering the sun and moderating its effects. High pressure and high clouds are perfect. Weather from the west tends to be wetter so easterly winds are good.

The more time you can spend on Skye prior to your traverse, the greater your chance of success. Not only can you wait for a suitable weather window but you can use the time to check out

some of the more complex sections of the ridge. People can and do turn up and jump straight on the ridge and can get lucky, but a longer visit is preferable.

May to September offers the best chance of success. The summer should bring better weather and longer hours of daylight but can be offset by a proliferation of midges. In mid summer, with clear skies, it virtually never gets completely dark and head torches will only be necessary from 11pm–4am.

Get into the habit of weather watching not just on Skye but when you are preparing for your trip. Compare forecasts to the actual weather on the ground either by looking out of the window if you are there or by looking at the various webcams (refer to Appendix B for links).

Weather forecasts are usually pretty good but remember they are just that, a forecast not a certainty etched in stone. Try not to get out of sync with the weather because you need to be ready to go as soon as a promising weather window is forecast. It is all very well getting out and practicing or exploring sections of the ridge in poor weather but you don't want to be tired out with soaking wet gear when the weather comes good.

XC Weather is favoured by the local fishermen and is also pretty good especially for wind directions and strengths for the next five days. Remember, it is for sea level and temperatures and wind speeds will be markedly different high on the ridge. Often the fishermen select 'Canna' to get an idea of the weather coming in from the west.

Met Office Mountain Forecast for the north-west Highlands covers a huge area but individual peaks in the Cuillin can be selected from a drop down choice on the area map. This forecast is usually pretty good with a high degree of accuracy. This is the preferred forecast of the author and on the whole it's very accurate. Very comprehensive and shows precipitation, wind speed, visibility, temperatures and more.

Mountain Weather Information Service (MWIS) also covers the north-west Highlands but has less specific Cuillin information than the Met Office where you can pinpoint relevant peaks.

Try and see as many different forecasts as possible and, if you are on Skye, try to correlate their accuracy to reality in the hills. Homework can be done in advance by following the different forecasts and comparing with what people actually experience and post about on social media.

Geology of the Black Cuillin

Skye with its range of different rock types, vulcanicity and subsequent glaciation is a geologist's dream location. Geologists have studied the Cuillin since the 1800s but their true importance was not recognised until Dr Alfred Harker mapped and interpreted them in the early 1900s.

The Black Cuillin is composed mainly of a very rough rock, gabbro, and finer grained basalt and dates from around 60 million years ago. These igneous rocks are the eroded remains of the magma chamber of a massive volcano. Roughly 12km across, the magma chamber has been exposed subsequently by glaciation and weathering.

Gabbro is the main building block of the Black Cuillin. It is a very coarse grained igneous rock and is typically grey, brown or black. Extremely rough, it is excellent to climb on but renowned for wearing out boots and fingertips. It consists largely of white, rectangular feldspar crystals, which are very resistant to erosion and thus stand proud of the surface of the rock and explain the rock's abrasive and frictional qualities. Formed from magma, gabbro cooled very slowly, deep in the earth, hence

The initial climb out from Bealach Mhic Choinnich to reach both King's Chimney and Collie's Ledge on a hot day (Section 4)

allowing time for the crystals to grow and its rough texture to form.

Peridotite is also an igneous rock but formed mostly from olivine, which is rich in iron and magnesium. Olivine weathers to a distinctive hue of orange-brown, which often contrasts with darker surrounding rocks. Peridotite often forms distinct layers within the gabbro and can often look reminiscent of egg boxes where hard white feldspar stands proud from the softer brown olivine. The classic location for peridotite is the head of Coir' a' Ghrunnda especially Caisteal a' Garbh-choire.

Basalt is also of volcanic origin but much smoother and finer grained. Its chemical composition is similar to gabbro but it is fine grained due to more rapid cooling. Much of the distinctive jagged shape of the Black Cuillin owes itself to the latter basalt intrusions through the gabbro. Smooth and fine grained, basalt can be treacherous in the wet but also facilitates ascents and descents with basalt dykes often forming very distinct staircase like features.

Basalt will be seen both in **dykes** and **cone sheets**. Dykes are usually up to a few metres thick and typical are the staircases on Bidein. Cone sheets are funnel shaped intrusions of basalt and can form ledges and slabs. Cone sheets are relatively thin (a few metres

Clockwise from bottom left: Periotite block below Caisteal a' Garbh-choire; Basalt dyke intruded through gabbro slabs in Coire Lagan, note the coarse gabbro versus the finer basalt; Basalt dyke staircase on West Peak of Bidein

The boat departs as a team prepares to ascend Gars-bheinn

thick) inclined sheets that look like a downward pointing cone. Cone sheets often form gently dipping but potentially slippery ledges. A typical example is Collie's Ledge on Sgurr Mhic Choinnich. The base of The Imposter on Clach Glas is a cone sheet and this continues as slab down the western flank.

Glaciation

The Cuillin was shaped by glaciation and at its height, Skye may have been under more than 1600m of ice. Various periods of glaciation effected the Cuillin but during the last glacial maximum, perhaps 18,000 years ago, an ice dome was centred on the Cuillin. Much of the Cuillin Ridge itself stood above the ice.

Lots of evidence of glaciation exist. The glacially smoothed slabs of Coire Lagan bear testament to the power of the ice. A terminal moraine exists below Coir' a' Ghrunnda and Loch Coruisk was scraped out by the passing of the glacier to a depth of 30m below sea level.

Logistics

Transport on Skye

Unless you have access to two cars, you may need to use public transport or hitch to retrieve parked cars especially if accessing the ridge from Elgol. Skye seems an easy place to hitch lifts especially on the Glen Brittle, Sligachan, Elgol triangle. I have often been picked up even when not hitching and been told, 'Don't be afraid to use the thumb'.

Buses are not that frequent and many are linked to ferrying school children. There are no buses to Glen Brittle, but there is one to Elgol from Broadford. Plan accordingly using the Traveline website, www.travelinescotland.com.

Taxis are expensive and can entail a long wait. Remember mobile reception is non-existent in many places (eg Glen Brittle) and poor elsewhere. It is good on much of the ridge so if you are sure of a time then you could risk phoning ahead and trusting to luck.

Boats trips from Elgol to the landing steps by the hut at Coruisk are £14 each way and are run by Misty Isle Boat Trips (http://mistyisleboattrips.co.uk).

Petrol
You can buy petrol 24 hours a day at the Co-op in Broadford, and it's usually the cheapest on the island. More expensive options are available at Portree and the Kyle of Lochalsh and elsewhere.

Shops etc
There is a largish Co-op in Broadford that is well stocked. Broadford also has a good bakery, cafés and pubs etc. There are no shops in Glen Brittle but the campsite does good coffee and has a shop selling basic provisions. There are no shops at the Sligachan but there are the Co-ops at Portree (and many other shops) or Broadford. Portree has

Inside Out, a gear shop, but it is only fairly small with a limited stock. It's good for emergency purchases and worth a look but it's best to arrive with all the kit you need.

Pubs
The Sligachan has a pub with lots of climbing history having been made by early climbers based here. The pub does meals and has accommodation, and the campsite and a bunkhouse are just opposite. Seumas' Bar is often full of climbers and walkers. It does great food and excellent cakes and stocks 450 different whiskies – definitely the place to celebrate finishing the ridge.

The Old Inn, Carbost, is small but recommended for its food and atmosphere, while Taigh Aileen at Portnalong is a bit off the beaten track but serves great food and is very friendly. Broadford has a variety of pubs and hotels.

Accommodation
Many climbers will opt for wild camping or either Glen Brittle or the Sligachan campsite. There are lots of laybys and places to park a van or car and you'll often see tents pitched by the roadside. Contact information for the places listed below can be found in Appendix B.

The **Sligachan Campsite** is open from April until October. It has good facilities, good showers and it's within walking distance to the pub. You can't book in advance but it does have a lot of space.

The **Glen Brittle Campsite** is open from April to September. It has an idyllic location by the beach with a

*Many climbers choose
to finish the ridge in the
Sligachan Hotel (pictured)
or Seumas' Bar next door*

backdrop of the Cuillin, and provides an on-site shop and café. The MWIS forecast is displayed daily in the café. Glen Brittle is perhaps the best base for the ridge. The only disadvantages are there is no mobile reception and no shops etc, so you need to arrive with everything you need.

Camasunary Bothy lacks the history or atmosphere of the old bothy but the new, purpose-built one is utilitarian and in a wonderful location and only an hour or so walk from the Elgol road. Best of all, it's free but it can get very busy with groups walking the Skye Trail etc.

Cloud inversion with view to Bla Bheinn from Sgurr nan Eag

Youth hostels are available in Glen Brittle and Broadford. Glen Brittle is perfectly located and displays the MWIS forecast daily in reception.

The **Glen Brittle Memorial Hut** has a lot of history and is fantastically located. It has three dormitories, each with six beds and has recently been extensively modernised. However, it is largely block-booked by clubs from May onwards.

The **Coruisk Hut** is owned by The Junior Mountaineering Club of Scotland. Fantastically located at Loch Coruisk, it has nine beds. It has walking and scrambling from the doorstep, and is accessible by foot or boat from Elgol.

Reasons for failure

Most teams that do not finish do so for a combination of reasons, the most significant revolving around running out of time or determination. The constant exposure and need to remain focused can become a psychological torture and it is all too easy to give in and seek escape. Escape is relatively easy and many succumb. The main reasons below all effect timing and as you slow down, the pressure piles on.

Whatever the reasons, learn from your mistakes. Some teams will have been sufficiently put off to never want to try again but the majority will see it as a challenge to return to for future success. It is, after all, a good reason to return to Skye and spend more time in the Cuillin. I met one person in the Glen Brittle Memorial Hut who has attempted the ridge eight times and is still to succeed, but what determination he must possess to keep on returning again and again.

Weather

The main factor is generally reduced visibility, which makes navigation much harder and slows forward progress. Wet rock is the other major effect of poor weather. Hot weather with searing sunshine can also be debilitating as you struggle over hard terrain, perhaps with too little water.

Navigation

Even with good visibility people make mistakes and take the wrong line and time can be lost. This can suggest a lack of concentration or a lack of preparation with not enough time spent practicing navigation and exploring the more complex parts of the ridge.

Fitness

Many teams underestimate the physicality of the challenge and turn up on spec not having put in the mileage.

The team

Some teams haven't practiced enough together and discrepancies and incompatibilities occurred. One member may have been far stronger than the other, or prepared to solo much more. Tempers may have become frayed and retreat was taken as the sensible choice.

Strategy and tactics

Perhaps the team opted for TRIAD when CREST would have been more suitable; possibly some of the technical climbing pitches should have been bypassed.

Beyond the ridge

The Black and Red Cuillin offer enough challenges to last a lifetime but there are a couple of bigger exploits that raise the level far above the Great Traverse.

The Greater Traverse

This takes in the Cuillin outliers and completes the circuit of the bowl formed by the Black Cuillin (20km and 4000m ascent). It requires a lot of stamina since the descent into Glen Sligachan takes you almost down to sea level followed by the consequent re-ascent to Clach Glas and the traverse to Bla Bheinn. The Clach Glas traverse is well worth doing in its own right (see Practice route 9) but even better as the grand finale to a Greater Traverse. Traditionally it doesn't include Sgurr na h-Uamha but logically and geologically their inclusion makes sense. It has been done in a day but more popular is a multi-day effort. It makes a splendid add on to a two-day ridge traverse and just means carrying a little extra food. If you start with the boat trip from Elgol it can be made into a circular route by descending Bla Bheinn's south ridge and following the coast path back to the start. It was first done in 1939 by IC Charleson and WE Forde in 20 hours peak-to-peak.

The Cuillin Round

This is a 'rock and run' challenge taking in 59 tops over 54km with more than 7000m of ascent. It visits 12 Munros, a dozen more Munro tops but avoids any hard technical climbing and was conceived as an unroped scramble to be done in under 24 hours. This round needs not only a very high level of fitness but a good knowledge of the Cuillin and an ability to solo things like the In Pinn. Clive Rowland was possibly the first person who completed the round (unsupported), in 31 hours in 1981 – in what he described as an 'unrecorded fun day'. Then, in the early 1980s, Eifon Jones and Rob David started from Sligachan and went round clockwise to Bla Bheinn, round the Bad Step, and along the Main Ridge (including T-D Gap and Sgurr Alasdair; excluding Sgurr Sgumain and Sgurrs Beag/Uamha) back to Sligachan to finish just inside the one-day mark. They were unsupported and carried a rope for the abseils. Calum Smith completed a solo and unsupported round in July 1991 in a 34-hour trip from Sligachan, which included a bivi on Sgurr na Banachdich. The fastest recorded round, which includes most of the major peaks of the Black and Red Cuillin, was done by Mark Shaw in July 2002. He started at Camasunary and went round clockwise in 16hr 46min.

The first person to complete a Super-Extended Greater Traverse (and in under 24 hours) was Rob Woodall. The route he took included Glamaig, the Deargs, Marsco (2 tops), Belig, Garbh-bheinn, Sgurr nan Each (2 tops), Clach Glas (2 tops), Bla Bheinn (2 tops), Sgurr

Hain, Sgurr na Stri, and all the Munros and Tops of the main Cuillin Ridge, plus many others including Sgurr Beag and Sgurr na h-Uamha: 59 tops in all (51km, 7000m of ascent). The round was completed on 31 May 1999 in a 23hr 28min (after a 1am start, paced/supported). The round is probably best tackled clockwise from the Coruisk Hut, but logistical problems meant that this trip

Looking down S Ridge of Sgurr a' Ghreadaidh towards Sgurr na Banachdich and even the In Pinn, top left (Section 6)

started in Glen Sligachan. The following year, Yiannis Tridimas (who had been one of the entourage who supported Rob in 1999) repeated the feat, and added an extra peak (Sgurr a' Bhasteir) in an impressive time of 21h 22min. The successful run (again paced/supported) took place in June 2000 with a midday start from the Coruisk Hut.

The Sligachan Horseshoe

Start at the Sligachan, ascend Glamaig then traverse the Red Cuillin to Marsco and then up Garbh-bheinn, Sgurr nan Each and the Clach Glas-Bla Bheinn traverse. Strangely Sgurr na Stri is bypassed via the Bad Step above Loch Scavaig and then the Main Ridge is followed back to the Sligachan. It is 45km with 6000m of ascent.

The Trans Cuillin Challenge

Here's your chance for fame since this hasn't yet been done. It's another 24-hour challenge, a west-to-east traverse taking every Cuillin top between Gars-bheinn and Beinn na Caillich. It includes everything with at least a 50ft drop all round and includes 70 tops (more than 61km with nearly 9000m of ascent).

Using this guide

This guide aims to help the reader complete the traverse of the Cuillin Ridge in summer conditions. The chapters progress towards this aim with additional chapters devoted to The Greater Traverse and The Winter Ridge.

The book is two volumes; the first helps you prepare for the ridge both before your arrival on Skye and after you arrive. Volume two has everything you need for your traverse of the ridge; a route description, map and photo topos. Points on the route are numbered and these numbers are consistent across the topos, maps and text.

Unless you are very experienced, it is suggested that some of the classic scrambles are done before the traverse itself. This will enable you to both recce parts of the ridge but also to get used to the terrain, the different rock types and the scale involved.

The 10 classic scrambles each have a summary information box that details the location, the grade, time, altitude and aspect and conditions. There is a lot of scope to use a practice route and

extend it to recce part of the ridge by using it in conjunction with the relevant section.

The winter ridge traverse (which has been described from north to south) has been divided into 10 sections. Each section has a map showing numbered waypoints along the route that correlate with numbers in the accompanying text and photo topos. In good visibility, the map and text may suffice, especially if the more complex sections have already been explored. However, it is best if the map, text and photo topos are all used in conjunction. Abseils and escape routes are marked on the maps.

The main route is marked in red with alternatives in green. Numbered waypoints (❶, ❷, ❸ etc) are sometimes subdivided further into Roman numerals (❶, ❷, ❸ etc).

Any instructions, left and right are assumed to be from facing the direction of travel (ie south to north). If there may be any confusion then additional instructions such as 'on Glen Brittle side' or on 'Loch Coruisk side' are added to clarify things.

All maps are reproduced from the Harvey Superwalker XT25 map, Skye: The Cuillin. It is recommended that you carry a hard copy of this map with you to provide an overview since each map section only covers a small area. A complete map also allows for change of plans should that be necessary. Many thanks to Harvey for agreeing to the use of their maps in this guide.

Classic scrambles

High above Loch Coruisk on the Dubh Slabs

Classic scrambles

These 10 routes (ordered approximately by grade) range from little more than tough walks through hard scrambles and easier graded climbs. They provide a variety of grades and offer opportunities both to explore the Cuillin and recce parts of the ridge. There are enough routes here for an extended trip to Skye and they provide both a chance to scope out the ridge for your traverse and a few routes for any spare time afterwards.

Many are great routes in their own right but most offer scope to explore parts of the ridge in preparation for a traverse. Thus the Dubh Ridge is a fantastic route, offers an alternative route up onto the ridge and could easily be combined with an exploration of the T-D Gap. Sgurr Thuilm and the NW Ridge of Sgurr a' Meadaidh can be done as a shortish trip or extended to explore the four tops of Mhadaidh and even to continue over Bidein. The routes can also give an indication of whether your are likely to achieve 'guidebook time' on the ridge traverse itself.

Some of the easier routes are good poor weather alternatives and all the routes provide fantastic views of the Cuillin, none more so than the diminutive summit of Sgurr na Stri.

Route 1
Round of Fionn Choire

Start	Park at the layby next to Skye Mountain Rescue Team's (MRT's) base (next door to the Sligachan Hotel)
Grade	1/2
Time	5–6hr
Altitude	Up to 958m (3145ft)
Aspect	Faces NW
Conditions	Fairly straightforward, being more of a walk than scramble, so a safe bet in less than ideal conditions.

With fantastic views, this route provides a good introduction to the northern end of the ridge. It can easily be added to other routes, such as checking out Naismith's Route or Lota Coire Route on the Bhasteir Tooth.

❶ Take the footpath on the opposite side of the road from the layby. Cross the first footbridge then ignore the second bridge and head right on the path along the river bank. Continue until below the entrance to the impressive **Bhasteir Gorge**.

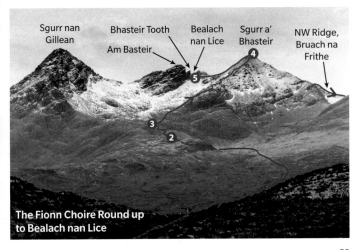

The Fionn Choire Round up to Bealach nan Lice

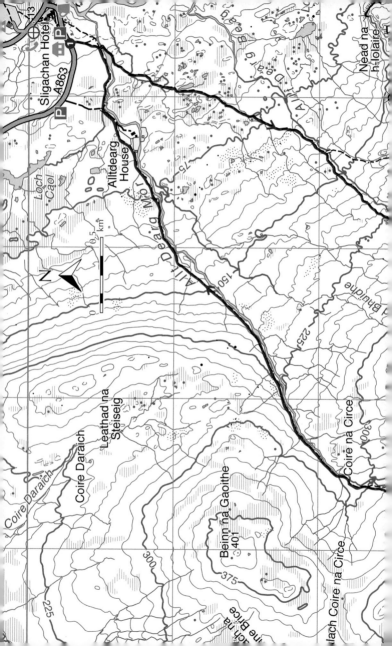

2 Ascend scree and slabby rocks W of the gorge entrance following obvious signs of wear.

3 NE ridge, Sgurr a' Bhasteir (1/2). Head up right, away from the gorge and follow the ridge. After some rough walking and easy scrambling, you will reach slabby rocks that lead to an obvious gully, which descends into **Coire a' Bhasteir** on the left. Continue to the summit of Sgurr a' Bhasteir.

4 From the summit, head S along a steep sided ridge with splendid views across to Sgurr nan Gillean, Pinnacle Ridge and **Am Basteir** on one side and Fionn Choire and Bruach na Frithe on the other. The ridge widens out and leads to **Bealach nan Lice** between Sgurr Fionn Choire and the **Bhasteir Tooth**.

5 From Bealach nan Lice, skirt below the rock of **Sgurr Fionn Choire** (or traverse it at 2/3) on a path and continue to reach the E ridge of Bruach na Frithe. Follow the ridge then head slightly left to reach the summit of Bruach na Frithe.

Sgurr nan Gillean

Bhasteir Tooth

Sgurr Fionn Choire

Bealach nan Lice

5

View from part way up
the E ridge, Bruach na Frith

On Bruach na Frithe's NW ridge

6 **NW ridge, Bruach na Frithe (2).** This is another ridge with fine views to both sides. For a more interesting descent, seek out a more direct line on the crest but difficulties can be bypassed by scree and faint paths to the left. The ridge leads down to **Bealach a' Mhaim.**

7 Follow the path on the N bank of the Allt Dearg Mor back towards Sligachan. Once you're past Allt Dearg, (the very obvious white cottage), follow the track then continue along the riverbank back to the MRT layby.

Route 2

The Spur, Sgurr an Fheadain

Start	Fairy Pools car park
Grade	2
Time	4–5hr
Altitude	Up to 688m (2255ft)
Aspect	Faces NW
Conditions	Although slabby, the holds are mainly very positive and it's viable in damp conditions.

This route involves easy scrambling, and enjoys views down to the famous Fairy Pools. It's a good poor weather alternative and is easily combined with a traverse of Bidein and can be made into a circular route by continuing along the ridge to Bruach na Frithe and descending its NW ridge.

High on The Spur, Sgurr a Fheadain

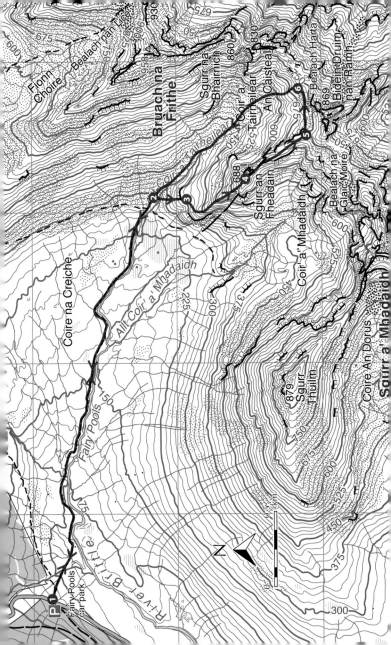

The Spur, Sgurr an Fheadain (2)

Coir' a' Mhadaidh

Waterpipe Gully

Sgurr an Fheadain **4**

3

Coir' a' Tairneilear

descent from Bealach Harta

2

1 From the car park, cross the road and follow the path up towards Sgurr an Fheadain heading up into **Coir' a' Tairneilear**.

2 Cross the stream and follow a faint path up right to reach slabby rocks forming the left side base of the ridge. Slabs of a go-anywhere nature provide enjoyable scrambling and lead to a levelling off.

3 Cut right across screes towards a very distinctive rowan tree and head up to the crest of the NW ridge, which you should follow more or less directly to the summit of Sgurr an Fheadain. **Waterpipe Gully** is visible on the right.

4 From the summit, descend on the right of the ridge, scrambling to broken rocks and a dip in the ridge that leads towards Bidein. Escape is possible on both sides with descents into either corrie but it's best to continue along the ridge, enjoying the fantastic views either side and to Bidein in front.

5 Decide whether to traverse left across scree slopes towards **Bealach Harta** before descending to the Fairy Pools or to carry on up the ridge and traverse Bidein (refer to Section 8 in the Topo booklet for description).

6 Descend screes below Bealach Harta then follow the stream down to return to the Fairy Pools' path and the car park.

Route 3
South South East Buttress, Sgurr na Stri

Start	Landing steps at Loch Coruisk
Grade	2/3
Time	It's 45min from the landing steps if you're catching a boat from Elgol; otherwise, a 2hr walk from Kilmarie. Allow 4–5hr for the round trip from boat to boat.
Altitude	Sea level to 494m (1620ft)
Aspect	Faces SSE
Conditions	Rough rock but well worth saving for a clear day since the summit views are one of the main reasons for the ascent.

A good scramble in an imposing position above the sea, this is very much a go-where-you-please route with the line open to much variation. The summit provides the best view of the Cuillin Ridge and it's a great place to put geographic reality to what you've seen and read about the Cuillin. The best approach is by Misty Isle Boat Trips from Elgol but it's also possible to walk along the coast path from Elgol or from Kilmarie.

❶ Follow the path inland from the landing steps and cross the River Scavaig (which flows out of Loch Coruisk) by stepping stones. Follow the coast path and negotiate **The Bad Step** where a slab of rock has to be crossed. Do not be lured into trying to cross it too high up. A horizontal ledge leads to a downward slanting crack in an exposed position. The descent is easier than it looks. Continue along the path until you can see the obvious gully above which splits the summit of Sgurr na Stri.

❷ Leave the coastal path and head diagonally up towards the ridge.

Close to the summit of Sgurr na Stri

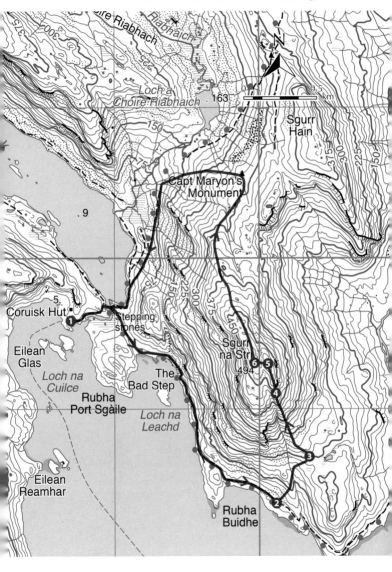

SSE ridge, Sgurr na Stri

Fantastic views from the SSE Buttress, Sgurr na Stri

❸ The route proper starts at around 150m by an obvious slab above a grassy saddle with a lochain to the E. Climb the slab then follow the easy ground up to the main rocky ridge, which leads to the summit. Pick your line and ascend lovely rock to reach a levelling off below the steeper summit rocks.

❹ It is possible to traverse easily into the gully and head up it to the summit. For more fun, head directly up to the E Summit.

❺ Descend into the horizontal depression splitting the summits then ascend to the W Summit with stunning views across **Loch Coruisk** to the Cuillin.

❻ Various options exist for the return to Coruisk. The obvious gully in the seaward face can be descended but make sure to take the western gully when it splits otherwise you will find your way barred by steep rocks. Better is to traverse **Sgurr na Stri** by descending NNW then heading NE to visit **Captain Maryon's Monument** before following the outflow from **Loch a' Choire Riabhaich** back to Loch Coruisk and so back to the landing steps.

Route 4
Thuilm Ridge, Sgurr a' Mhadaidh

Start	Park opposite Glen Brittle Youth Hostel
Grade	3 (or Moderate if slab is taken)
Time	5–6hr
Altitude	Up to 918m (3010ft)
Aspect	NW facing
Conditions	Fairly straightforward and, apart from the slab, doable in damp conditions.

This fine ridge has fantastic views on either side and several good reasons for doing it. A good scramble in its own right, it can be combined with a recce of the four tops of Mhadaidh and the three tops of Bidein, the most complicated part of the whole ridge. It can also be combined with dropping off food or water for your ridge traverse since An Dorus is the notional half-way point.

❶ Follow the path up towards **Coire a' Ghreadaidh**. At about 367m, cross the **Allt a' Choire Ghreadaidh** and head towards Sgurr Thuilm.

❷ You can ascend the SW flank of Sgurr Thuilm without scrambling. For more sport, seek out The Black Slab (Moderate), which provides access via the SW Buttress. Continue to the summit.

Looking back to summit of Sgurr Thuilm from below the crux slab

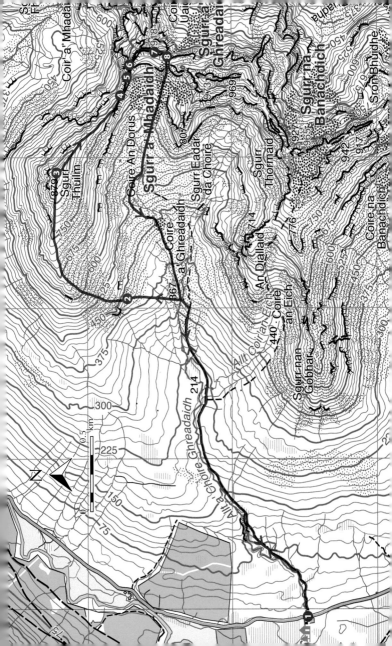

Sgurr a' Ghreadaidh

Sgurr a' Mhadaidh 918m

Coire An Dorus

NW ridge of Sgurr a' Mhadaidh

Third top

Second top

First top

Bidein 869m

Coir' a' Mhadaidh

Crux slab on Thuilm ridge, Sgurr a' Mhadaidh

3 From the summit, descend the SE ridge of Sgurr Thuilm (1) to reach the **NW ridge of Sgurr a' Mhadaidh**.

4 Scramble up the ridge crest to arrive at a large slab to the left of a distinctive, wide chimney.

5 The best route involves traversing right across the slab (Moderate) on good rock but it is possible to avoid the slab by sticking to the left of the buttress lower down; go up the left side of the ridge, scramble awkwardly past a recess then return to the right of the ridge.

6 Follow the ridge in a more straightforward fashion, pass a steep step then the impressive in-cut of Deep Gash Gully, which comes in from the left. After a small levelling off, go right then up a chimney/groove and continue rightwards to the summit of Sgurr a' Mhadaidh.

7 **SW ridge, Sgurr a' Mhadaidh (2/3)**. Descend from the summit slab and scramble down short steps and rocks leading to the steep-sided An Dorus, which bisects the ridge.

8 Carefully, climb down into An Dorus then down slabby rocks and scree to **Coire An Dorus**.

9 Follow the stream down, staying on the N bank before crossing to the S at about 370m, then continue on the good path back to the road.

Route 5
South Ridge, Sgurr Coir' an Lochain

Start	Park at Glen Brittle Memorial Hut
Grade	Difficult
Time	6–7hr
Altitude	759m (2490ft), but you have to go over the higher Bealach Mhic Choinnich
Aspect	N facing
Conditions	Mainly a rugged walk so doable in any weather but the whole point is about its remote location and views so it's best saved for a half decent day.

Reputedly the last mountain summit to be climbed in the UK, this route is mostly a long walk with a climb/scramble but it's a remote peak in a stunning location. It can easily be combined with checking out King's Chimney/Collie's Ledge on Sgurr Mhic Choinnich and/or a recce of the line of the descent from Sgurr Thearlaich to Bealach Mhic Choinnich. For a really long day, consider doing the route, descending to Coruisk and returning via the Dubh Ridge.

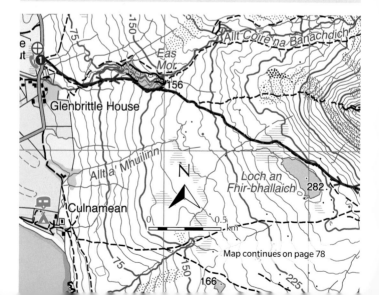

Map continues on page 78

Sgurr Alasdair
Sgurr Mhic Choinnich
Sgurr na Banachdaich
Sgurr a' Ghreadaidh

3

4

South Ridge, Sgurr Coir' an Lochain

❶ Follow the path up past **Eas Mor** and up into Coire Lagan.

❷ Ascend the start of the **Great Stone Chute** but branch off left to reach Bealach Mhic Choinnich.

❸ From the bealach, descend rocks and scree but stay over to the left (Mhic Choinnich) side. Continue over an awkward rock step and more scree to awkward slabs best descended on the left. Then cross the easier terrain that leads down to the crest leading out to **Sgurr Coir' an Lochain**.

❹ The ridge is a straightforward walk out to the last top (759m) before a small gap separates the main ridge from a further small top, which is splendidly isolated with drops on three sides.

Descending the crux into the gully before the summit of Sgurr Coir' an Lochain

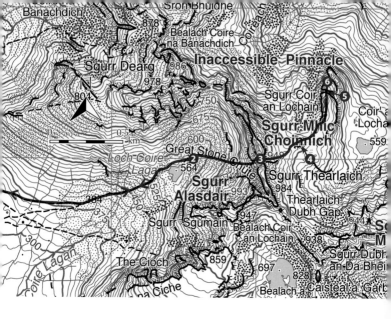

⑤ The crux is down-climbing into the gap. An easier scramble out leads to the furthest top.

⑥ Unusually this northern most top is accepted as the summit despite being lower than points on the S ridge.

Return by same route.

If making it a long day before combining with the Dubh Ridge (Classic scramble 6) then retrace the route almost to waymark 4, descend to Coir an Lochain and then Loch Coruisk before starting the Dubh Ridge.

Route 6
The Dubh Ridge

Start	Landing steps at Loch Coruisk
Grade	Moderate, plus abseil
Time	7hr 30min–8hr 30min (start/finish at landing steps at Loch Scavaig/Coruisk)
Altitude	Sea level to 944m.
Aspect	Ridge faces east.
Conditions	A slabby route best done in the dry.
Approaches	The easiest approach by far is to catch The Misty Isle Boat from Elgol. It is then only a 1.5km walk to the base of the ridge. If you are fast, catch the boat from Elgol, race up and return by the last boat. If not, then consider camping or staying at the JMCS Hut Coruisk Hut). It is possible to walk in from Elgol or Kilmarie (if the boats are not running) or from Glen Brittle via Bealach Mhic Choinnich, Coir' an Lochain or Garbhh choire.

This route offers superb slab climbing high above Loch Coruisk, followed by an airy ridge to a Munro tick. This makes a good training day but has little specific recce value for your ridge traverse. However, if transport arrangements allow then this can be extended to recce the ridge along to the Thearlaich Dubh Gap (T-D Gap) and beyond. It is surprisingly committing for such a lowly graded route with it being fairly remote and reasonably inescapable. Note a 60m rope will be required for the 30m abseil.

❶ Follow the path from Coruisk until below the bulk of the ridge where the path is close to the loch's edge.

❷ Ascend a grassy gully to reach a flat shoulder after 75m. This gully can't be seen on the walk in until below the route.

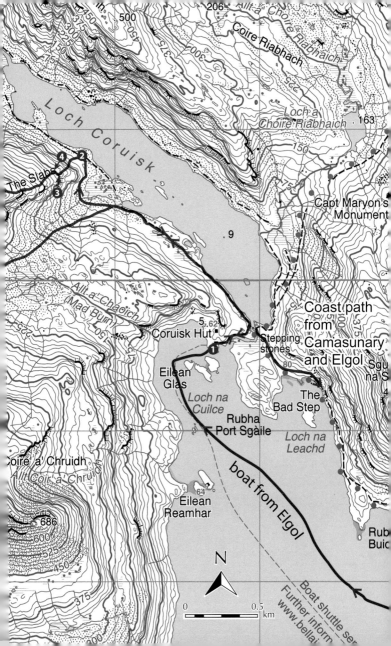

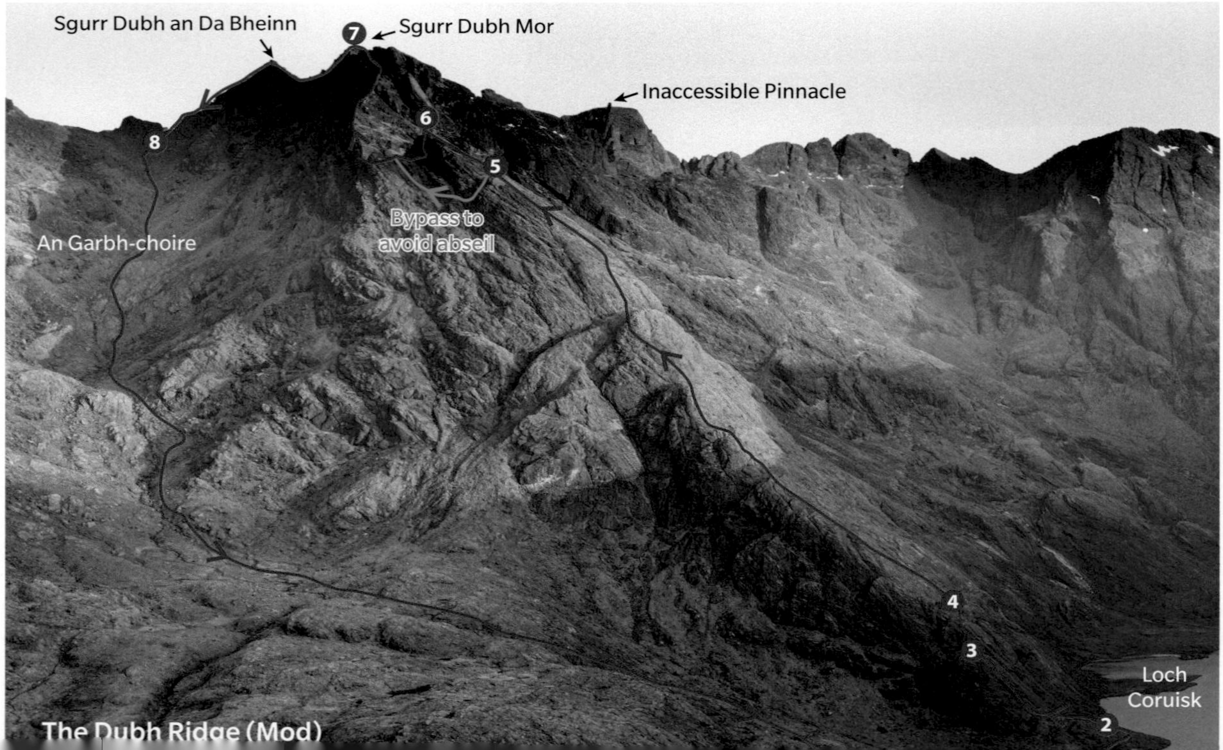
Sgurr Dubh an Da Bheinn
7
Sgurr Dubh Mor
Inaccessible Pinnacle
6
8
5
Bypass to avoid abseil
An Garbh-choire
4
3
Loch Coruisk
2
The Dubh Ridge (Mod)

❸ Climbing the steep band above and right of the gully is the crux of the whole route. From the flat shoulder above the gully, climb a series of blocky steps starting from a leaning block and go up and left with a couple of awkward moves before cutting right on to the crest of the ridge.

❹ The slabs are now of a go anywhere nature, a veritable pick-and-mix but generally, stick close to the left edge. Scramble up, pass two small terraces and you will arrive at a grassy hollow at 470m (possible escape route down and to the E). The slabs now become steeper with a choice of corner lines to take. Continue until 650m where a horizontal area offers the option of continuing to the summit or bypassing it.

❺ Continue fairly easily to reach the summit of **Sgurr Dubh Beag**.

You can bypass the summit by descending a short south-facing gully on scree. Cross broken rocks to a grassy ramp, which runs parallel to the ridge; follow the ramp until just before it narrows; and descend onto scree which leads to the down-climb below the abseil.

    This bypass does miss the summit but has the potential to save up to an hour so can be useful especially if you want to solo the ridge without a rope or you are with someone who is nervous about abseiling.

---

❻ Scramble down from the summit of Sgurr Dubh Beag to a large block, which is usually festooned with abseil slings. After an awkward take off, you'll abseil S to a grassy ledge. The abseil is almost 30m, much of it free-hanging, so a 60m rope is necessary. There is a lower anchor so it is possible to make two short abseils if your rope is too short. Then, make a short down-climb to get to the col at the head of **Coir' a' Chaoruinn** (another possible escape route. If time is short, it is possible also to escape from below the abseil down into An Garbh-choire by carefully picking your way down to the SE. This makes for a very fast descent if you need to get back to boat.).

    E ridge, Sgurr Dubh Mor (3) is a real contrast to the Dubh Slabs. From the foot of the abseil, head west then scramble (2) down a corner to reach a wide arete. Follow the arete to its end where a climb down a steep wall (3) leads to a col between Sgurr Dubh Beag and Sgurr Dubh Mor. After this, absorbing scrambling on the crest and easy ledges to its left will take you to the steep summit ridge, which can be taken direct but is quite hard and the rock is loose. Most teams choose to take the grassy ramps on the S. These provide a series of easier lines

The go anywhere nature of the Dubh Slabs means harder variations can be sought out

but all finish with a steep rock pitch just below the summit ridge, except the route furthest to the left.

You'll reach the ridge towards its eastern end and traverse the narrow ridge with steep drops off to the left. Make a sharp turn back left and go down steeply before following the final part of the ridge along mossy rocks to the summit at its western end.

7 SW spur, Sgurr Dubh Mor (2/3). See Section 2 in the Topo' Booklet for detailed topo. Scramble down to the col at the foot of the SW spur.

E ridge, Sgurr Dubh an Da Bheinn (2) has easy scrambling to the summit.

S ridge, Sgurr Dubh an Da Bheinn (2) is an enjoyable descent on very rough rocks. Stay close to the crest but slightly towards the Coir' a' Ghrunnda side. At the base of the ridge a tunnel under a rock just before the towering bulk of **Caisteal a' Garbh-choire** provides an escape route into **Coir' a' Ghrunnda**.

8 Descend into **An Garbh-choire** and down to **Loch Coruisk**. This is hard going over blocks and scree at first but eases off lower down where there are signs of a path on the N bank of the stream.

Follow the loch side back to the landing steps.

Route 7

Round of Coire Lagan

Start	Park at the Glen Brittle Memorial Hut
Grade	Difficult
Time	10hr
Altitude	Sea level to 993m (3260ft)
Aspect	The coire itself faces W
Conditions	It's worth saving such a classic for good conditions, especially as some parts of it will be much harder in the wet. The upper slabs on Sgurr Mhic Choinnich are basalt and will be treacherous if wet.
Note	Refer to Sections 3, 4 and 5 in the topo booklet for additional topos and description

This classic Cuillin coire round ticks many quality climbs, has extensive scrambling opportunities and provides a long training day. Completing it allows you to cover some crucial ground on the ridge and allows for a detailed recce of the tricky descent from Sgurr Thearlaich. More detail can be found in the Topo Booklet, Sections 3, 4 and 5.

1 Follow the path up past **Eas Mor** waterfall.

2 Ignore a minor turning on the left (this will be the way back from the Inaccessible Pinnacle (In Pinn) later) and continue past **Loch an Fhir-bhallaich**. Cross the path leading from Glen Brittle to Coire Lagan.

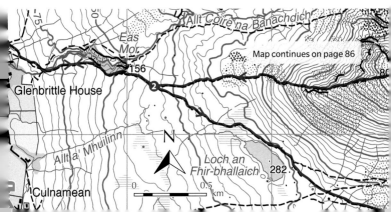

Map continues on page 86

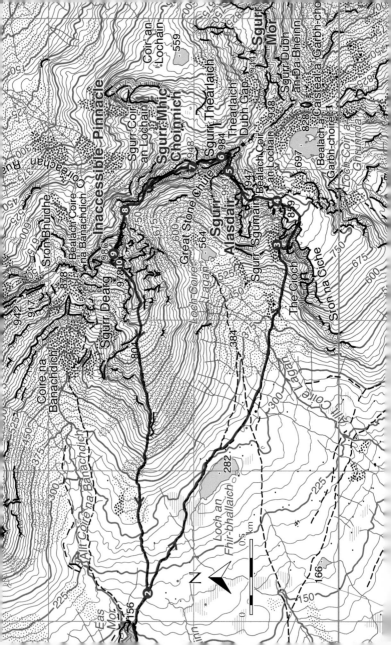

Sron na Ciche

The Cioch

3

Loch Coire Lagan

The Coire Lagan Round Part 1

Continue until below Sron na Ciche – the climb starts a long way up the screes. Pass up past a prominent scoop caused by rockfall to reach an obvious traverse back right along a cone sheet.

3 **The Terrace (Moderate, 150m).** This is used to access the base of the Cioch Slab. Scramble up and right on polished rock to a broad terrace, which soon narrows. Traverse more polished basalt past two noses above steep terrain before the fault leads into the boulder filled **Eastern Gully**. Exit the Eastern Gully by basalt slabs, which are often wet. It takes a few delicate moves to reach the terrace below the imposing Cioch Slab.

Collie's Route, the Cioch

Eastern Gully

The Shelf

The Cioch

Terrace

Eastern Gully

3

Collie's Route, Sron na Ciche (Moderate, 200m). Start 15m down and left of Slab Corner, the obvious intersection of the Cioch Slab and The Cioch itself. An obvious wide crack slants up left from the terrace. The climbing is easy and well protected but in an intimidating position high above the gully. After 50m, you'll reach ledges.

When the rock steepens, rejoin the Eastern Gully via easy blocks, then ascend the gully. There has been a large rock fall and there are big, precariously balanced blocks on the right edge of Eastern Gully. Ascend the gully and traverse right on slabs to a break known as The Shelf, which runs along the top of the Cioch Slab. Descend to **The Cioch** by an exposed rib called The Neck. Either step boldly across the nape of The Neck and climb up onto The Cioch with easier moves leading to the summit, or traverse 3m left (W) from the neck and then climb a chimney. This is less exposed but a marginally harder. There are usually in situ slings and most people choose to abseil rather than down-climbing to The Neck.

Return to Eastern Gully and ascend to an enormous chockstone, which must be passed by a claustrophobic squirm. Take the right fork higher up and continue until you emerge on the SW flank of Sron na Ciche. Continue easily to the summit of **Sron na Ciche** at 859m and then scramble down to Bealach a Coir' a' Ghrunnda.

Sword fight on The Cioch

The Coire Lagan Round Part 2

❹ S ridge, Sgurr Sgumain (walk). You'll mainly just need to walk over rough, rocky terrain to reach the summit of Sgurr Sgumain

NE ridge, Sgurr Sgumain (2/3). Descend past a small 'window' and continue down by interesting scrambling mostly just right of the crest to reach Bealach Sgumain with its distinctive pinnacles.

❺ SW flank, Sgurr Alasdair (3). Leave the bealach and head for a chimney 50m to the E and 20m lower down. Scramble up the polished 25m chimney and climb the left wall (crux) before making an exit to the right. Either zigzag up the shallow scoop above, and follow it to the summit of Sgurr Alasdair or, better still, cut back left to the narrow SW ridge, which is followed in fine positions to the summit.

SE ridge, Sgurr Alasdair (2). Descend the short steps and slabs to the top of the Great Stone Chute. The way is well worn and is exposed with spectacular views to the Stone Chute below and the ridge ahead.

❻ S Ridge, Sgurr Thearlaich (3). Descend from the top of the chute to the right (towards Coir' a' Ghrunnda) then follow distinctive strata that leads horizontally onto the ridge. Having regained ridge, carry on up towards the summit. When the ridge narrows, move on to its right (eastern) side. Enjoyable grade 3 scrambling will take you to the summit.

N Ridge, Sgurr Thearlaich (Moderate). Descend roof-like slabs from the summit of Sgurr Thearlaich, cross one gap in the crest and continue along to a second gap.

ⓘ Just beyond the second gap, descend to the right (E) and following slight signs of a path, which has general wear and tear. This is about 100m before the steep nose above Bealach Mhic Choinnich. Go around a corner to the left and along the ledges to the crux

ⓘⓘ The 10m wall is an awkward down-climb but only Moderate, if dry. Slings are occasionally in situ where people have abseiled. This is very exposed with huge drops below so, if in doubt, use a rope.

ⓘⓘⓘ Follow ledges below to another, easier and shorter down-climb. This leads to another ledge below that leads around and down to the bealach. The descent is exposed and sometimes there is a threaded sling in situ.

Next, you have a choice of a classic climb or an exposed walk/scramble. King's Chimney and Collie's Ledge both have the same start to exit the bealach.

From Bealach Mhic Choinnich, move 6m right (E) to a slab and short corner. Climb steeply, but on good holds, to gain the obvious traverse line of Collie's Ledge, which leads back left.

Coire Lagan Round Part 3 (view from Sgurr Alasdair)

In Pinn **9** **10**

An Stac Direct

An Stac bypass **8**

Sgurr Mhic Choinnich

Collie's Ledge

King's Chimney **7**

An Stac Screes

Sgurr Thearlaich

7 **King's Chimney, Sgurr Mhic Choinnich (Very Difficult, 25m)**. This is more corner than chimney and a classic that should not be missed if conditions and time allow. It's also easier than it looks, as long as it's dry. Rock 6 and Rockcentric 3 are useful, as are 120cm slings for the chockstones.

Scramble up the obvious, steep ramp going right from the start of the traverse of Collie's Ledge to:

i Belay on a ledge below the corner.

ii Climb the wide corner/crack on good gabbro passing chockstones (good threads).

iii Traverse out right on good but well-spaced holds to outflank the overhang.

iv Finish more easily.

v Arrive at a block belay with a good view down the route. Follow the exposed crest N for around 55m to the summit.

Collie's Ledge (Moderate). Providing sensational positions as you traverse high above Coire Lagan, this is a relatively easy route across improbable looking terrain. It's a good alternative to King's Chimney and fast since, hopefully, a rope will not be necessary.

Leaving the bealach by a short, steep climb is the crux and from then on, it is mostly walking with easy but very exposed scrambling. Continue under King's Chimney along a rising traverse line to reach an exposed nose where the route crosses the W buttress.

After turning a corner, go down to a scree path interspersed with a couple of short scrambles. Cross another nose of rock, then delicately traverse a steep rock band and continue easily to a distinctive chimney, which marks the junction with the N ridge. Follow the N ridge to the summit.

N ridge, Sgurr Mhic Choinnich (3). A narrow, beautifully situated ridge, it is slippery if wet (especially the upper basalt section). Initially very exposed, it gets easier as you descend. Descend 200m to just below a small rise where Collie's Ledge enters from the left. Continue down fairly easily, then scramble over blocks and go down grooves. Make sure to descend far enough to outflank the in-cut of Rotten Gully, then ascend to a plateau and cross to Bealach Coire Lagan.

8 **An Stac Direct, (3, 250m)**. This section provides impressive scrambling up the longest single vertical section of the whole ridge. It is a serious undertaking and inescapable, although its reputation for loose rock has been exaggerated. Not

Abseil from In Pinn

to be underestimated, it is increasingly steep and exposed and should only be undertaken by confident scramblers.

i Ascend an obvious ramp 10m left (S) of the crest and just beyond a notch at the NW end of the bealach. This dyke is typical of much of the route.

ii Cross easy terrain to an obvious U-shaped notch in the ridge to your right.

iii Scree slopes left of the notch offer a last chance to escape; otherwise, the only way is up. Climb a dyke/chimney just left of the crest to another, smaller notch.

iv The crest above is narrow and steepens. Traverse left to access the crest, and follow it for about 80m to where An Stac Chimney joins from the left. You'll be very exposed but on good holds.

v Follow the obvious chimney to its top.

vi Above the chimney, the terrain levels off. Traverse left then up easy corners to the summit. Descend easily and pass a stone bivi circle to reach the base of the In Pinn (3).

An Stac Bypass (2). This is a much easier alternative, which is especially useful if time or weather dictates avoiding the direct route. It follows an orange coloured ramp and screes and, being faster, provides the chance for you to overtake parties before the bottleneck of the In Pinn.

From Bealach Coire Lagan, descend rock steps and scree to an obvious path going up screes below the bulk of An Stac. Carry on in the same line up slabs, rocks and screes. Pass through a gap by some large boulders, veer right and then scramble up to a higher ramp line and continue up to the base of the In Pinn.

---

9 **E ridge, In Pinn (Moderate, 65m).** Start near the eastern end of the S face. Climb a broken chimney and go up along a ramp parallel to the E ridge to a possible belay.

i Leave the possible belay and gain the ridge and just above is the crux of the climb where the ridge briefly steepens. A very exposed couple of moves can be protected by a sling on a small spike. Better holds will soon appear and the more usual belay at 30m is reached. This is a ledge on the Coruisk side with large spike and block belays.

The In Pinn from summit ridge of Sgurr Dearg

(ii) Above the belay, things are easier and the ridge widens out. Belay on blocks overlooking a ledge that leads around the Bolster Stone (technically the highest point).

Descent of In Pinn (abseil). Follow the ledge right of the Bolster Stone to in situ maillons. The usual descent is to abseil the W ridge. Skilled climbers may choose to down-climb this (Severe). A 35m rope doubled will reach the ground. Most hold-ups occur with people queuing to abseil, so try and think outside the box. Use other anchors and get other people to throw your sling down or share ropes with other parties. Work with other parties.

Head up the slabs to the ridge that overlooks the In Pinn.

(10) The **W Ridge, Sgurr Dearg (1/2)**, provides beautiful views across Coire Lagan to the summits you've traversed. From the In Pinn, descend the ridge first on the right then cross to the left. You can go to the summit of the minor peak, Sgurr Dearg Beag or contour round to the left or right and then scramble down steeper ground to about 800m where the ridge levels off.

Continue down the now easier angled ridge, staying to the left. Don't be tempted to descend to the right but continue to almost the western end of the ridge where paths come up just right of the crest. Follow the path and scree down to meet an ever improving path that leads back past the Eas Mor waterfall and back to the Glen Brittle Memorial Hut.

Route 8
Pinnacle Ridge, Sgurr nan Gillean

Start	Layby next to Skye MRT's base
Grade	Mainly grade 3 scrambling, with a few Difficult moves and an abseil
Time	6hr 30min–7hr 30min
Altitude	600–965m (1970–3165ft)
Aspect	Ridge faces NE, so can be a good option in strong SW winds due to being in the lee of the bulk of Sgurr nan Gillean.
Conditions	A classic route best saved for good conditions but quite possible in the damp

This route is classic Cuillin climbing, with lots of scrambling, an abseil or two and the chance to recce the route you may be descending after your ridge traverse. It involves lots of top quality rock and exposure but, as with most mountain routes, it also has its share of loose rock. It's not a route to underestimate as it sees its share of epics. It's not ridge-specific unless you are planning to use it as a descent from Sgurr nan Gillean, but it can be extended to recce Am Basteir by the E ridge or, better still, via Naismith's or the Lota Corrie Route.

❶ Take the footpath opposite the Mountain Rescue base at Sligachan on the A863.

❷ At the first footbridge, cross the river.

❸ At the second footbridge cross the river and continue for about 1km to a huge cairn.

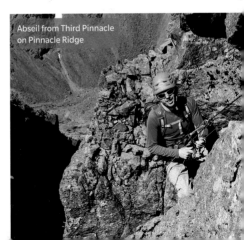

Abseil from Third Pinnacle on Pinnacle Ridge

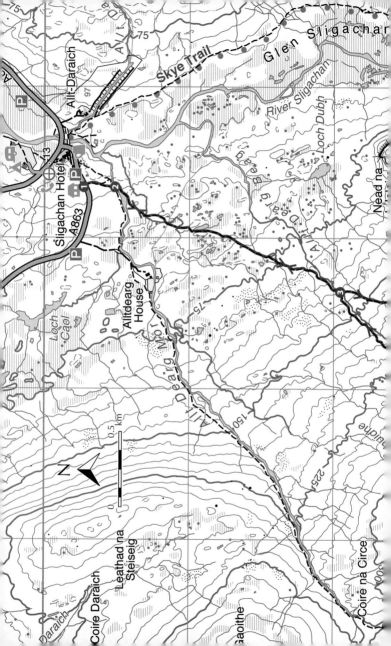

Pinnacle Ridge, Sgurr nan Gillean (Dif)

First Pinnacle

Second Pinnacle

Third Pinnacle

Knight's Peak

Sgurr nan
Gillean 965m

④ Ignore the continuation of the main path and turn right on a less obvious path, heading SW up onto the broad shoulder above the Bhastier Gorge. Follow this shoulder, which becomes more rocky and leads to the base of the First Pinnacle.

⑤ Start at the lip of **Coire a' Bhasteir** below the obvious mass of the First Pinnacle. Ascend the First Pinnacle's NW face by cutting left on easy ground. Go up a grassy groove and across slabs until above Black Chimney where the route cuts back right and follows a rake to the crest of the buttress. Continue slightly further right then go up a groove. Cut sharply left on a ledge and then go up a narrow basalt dyke/ chimney which enables steeper rocks to be overcome. Cross easier terrain to a horizontal section of the crest, then cross to the right side of the crest, and climb a block and a groove to regain to the ridge line. Continue up an *arête* then carry on with a gully to your right. Go slightly left and after a while the terrain levels out and you'll reach the summit of the **First Pinnacle**.

⑥ Descend from the First Pinnacle to the gully that separates it from the Second Pinnacle, turn right and cross slabs. Scramble to the summit of the **Second Pinnacle**. A far easier option is to head slightly left then a walk leads to the gap between the Second and Third Pinnacles.

Go up screes to where the rock steepens and leads up towards the Third Pinnacle. A short gully of light coloured rock divides the Third Pinnacle from a small tower to the right. Head up this gully before heading left and up rocky steps before continuing up broken terrain to a steep groove right of the ridge. This groove has obvious signs of wear and a crack/corner leads to a spectacular summit with drops all around.

⑦ **Third Pinnacle**. The majority of people use the in situ chain for an abseil. A 50m rope doubled will get you all the way down but it can done with a 40m rope, which will get you past the difficulties and the lower part can be down-climbed. However, if you have a 60m rope it will get you all the way down to the gap between the Third Pinnacle and Knight's Peak.

The abseil is one of the highlights of the route but it can be bypassed. From below the small tower at the base of the Third Pinnacle, make a traverse to the left of the Third Pinnacle on grass and scree to reach the gully separating the Third Pinnacle from Knight's Peak. Ascend the gully then descend on the Coire a' Bhasteir side to rejoin the route.

From the gap at the base of the abseil/down-climb, go right along an obvious ledge to the W for 30m, crossing two gaps and passing a large block. This obvious ramp line is initially very exposed. Go around a corner then cut back diagonally left to the ridge and follow a distinctive orange ramp then a leftward groove leads to blocks in a col below the twin tops of Knight's Peak. The N top is marginally higher.

❽ The descent from **Knight's Peak** is by sustained scrambling and the occasional presence of slings is evidence that some people choose to abseil. Knight's Peak is joined to the main summit of Sgurr nan Gillean via a ridge with two towers that stick up.

From the col below the twin peaks, head along a horizontal ledge then scramble down a slab/wall to reach a gap with a small tower ahead. Descend to the right, following signs of wear and a bit of a path in places. Zigzag to find the easiest line. From a grass ledge, cut back left on ledges to rejoin the ridge at a gap before the second tower. Go down right (Coire a' Bhasteir side) to skirt under the tower then cut back left to a gap (876m).

The climb from this gap is the crux of the whole ridge (assuming you abseiled rather than down-climbed from the Third Pinnacle) and is unavoidable. Awkward moves are required to reach the slabs above the gap. Various options exist, the easiest being to step leftwards using a high foothold and a long reach for a handhold to reach a crevassed block.

Go right then cut back left to reach a slabby recess 40m above with a chimney to its left. The rock above is taken direct to reach a terrace below yet another buttress which can also be taken direct but be careful of rock which is very loose. Another terrace is reached and the best way to finish is up a basalt dyke for 15m. This leads to the W ridge just below the summit. For an easier alternative, it is possible to traverse right from below the chimney along a terrace/ledge to reach the W ridge.

❾ **Descend by the W ridge, Sgurr nan Gillian** (grade 2 scramble and section of Moderate climbing, but the latter is usually abseiled). Leave the summit and head for the obvious pinnacle with a window through which you pass. Descend a volcanic pipe of weird, concrete like rock.

Scramble and walk down to the large block above Tooth Chimney, which usually has an array of abseil slings. The abseil is longer than a 35m rope doubled so take care and knot the rope ends. A 50m rope is necessary to reach the ledge.

Abseil from Third Pinnacle on Pinnacle Ridge as seen from Knight's Peak

A 35m rope will get you past the main difficulties and it's fairly easy to scramble down to the ledge. The abseil can be missed by descending the airy ridge, passing the remains of a missing pillar and down-climbing Easy Chimney (Moderate). Follow the ledge and retrace your route to Bealach a' Bhasteir.

🔟 From Bealach a' Bhasteir, descend loose screes to the N and down into **Coire a' Bhasteir**. Unless you are familiar with the route, keep your eyes open for signs of a path and general wear and tear. Take care on the descent of slabs to the W of the **Bhasteir Gorge** and be aware of the big drop on your right into the gorge.

Once below the gorge, it's an easy but long walk on a path, which improves as you get closer to the **Sligachan**.

Route 9
Clach Glas – Bla Bheinn Traverse

Start	Park at the car park on the edge of the forestry on the Broadford to Elgol road (GR 561 216)
Grade	Sustained scrambling and climbing to Difficult
Time	6hr 30 min–7hr 30min
Altitude	450–928m (1475–3045ft)
Aspect	Sgurr nan Each faces E; on main traverse of Clach Glas, there is a N facing ridge to ascend and S facing ridge to descend.
Conditions	Slabs will be unpleasant in the wet as will down-climbing the Imposter but, with care, the experienced will be able to do the traverse in less than perfect conditions. Route finding is intricate so not recommended in poor visibility.

One of the best mountaineering routes in the UK, Clach Glas is Scotland's answer to the Matterhorn. The route provides stunning views across Glen Sligachan to the main Cuillin Ridge and is usually combined with a traverse of Sgurr nan Each to make a horseshoe route around Coire a Caise. It's of no use for learning the main ridge but a fantastic route in its own right, and good training.

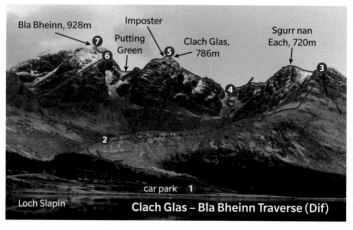

Clach Glas – Bla Bheinn Traverse (Dif)

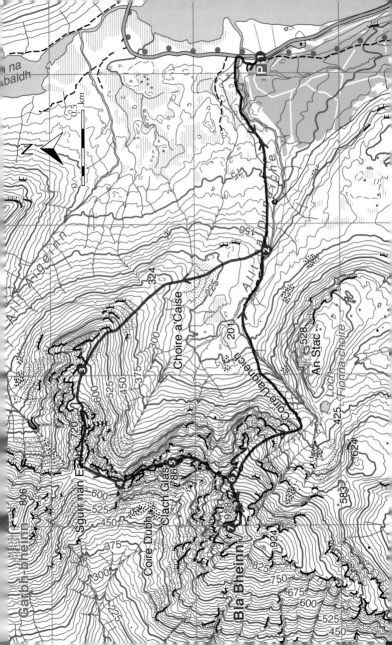

N ridge, Clach Glas (Mod)

❶ Cross the river to the north and take footpath on its northern bank. Follow the path up past several waterfalls.

❷ Turn right to reach the SE shoulder of Sgurr nan Each. Gain the eastern end of the summit ridge via scrambling up small outcrops of rock higher up.

❸ For the **traverse of Sgurr nan Each (1/2)**, leave the eastern end of the summit ridge and continue to the minor top above the north buttress before descending to follow a wide, grassy ridge and then rocky terrain to arrive at the main summit.

From the summit descend to the left of obvious rock fins to reach a steep slabby wall that guards the col below. Either down-climb an obvious slab left of the steep wall to reach a crack that leads down to the col (2/3), or bypass the slab to the left. Descend leftwards down less steep terrain then cut back right to the col (1/2). Follow easier terrain to the western top.

Descend to the levelling off between Surr nan Each and Garbh-bheinn then head S towards Clach Glas.

The N ridge of Clach Glas can be accessed more directly and faster via scree at the head of Choire a'Caise, which leads to the bealach between Clach Glas and Sgurr nan Each.

---

❹ **N ridge Clach Glas (Moderate).** In a nutshell, Clach Glas can be traversed using the following simple mantra; on the ascent, turn all difficulties to the right and on the descent turn them to the left. Clach Glas is very complex terrain and it is best to either continue on or return the way you have come rather than trying to escape down the steep flanks.

Leave the bealach below the ridge, ascend slabs and follow the ridge. A steep wall bars further progress and requires a 10m climb down steeply towards Loch Slapin then traverse back into the gap in the ridge. Continue along the ridge with much variation possible on the right.

ⓘ Descend into a wide scree-filled gully before the final summit block. This heralds the start of the harder climbing to reach the summit. Exit the gully by a v-shaped chimney/groove, which requires some awkward bridging. Either continue awkwardly up the chimney or avoid the upper part by a crack on the right, which leads out onto the ridge and up a rib to a platform.

ⅱ From the platform at the top of the chimney/rib, go up steeply **a** then right past an **b** overhang. Continue traversing right (sometimes over a distinctly wet streak **c**) then ascend before contouring back left and up to reach a squat pinnacle (possible belay **d**). Go behind the pinnacle and make a few moves up the narrow cleft between it and the headwall before breaking out onto the slabs on the right. Head straight up slabs before trending right to the summit.

gully behind squat pinnacle *(possible belay)*
d

distinctive roof

b

c

often damp

a

View from platform at top of v chimney looking up to Clach Glas summit block

5 S ridge, Clach Glas (Moderate). Leave the summit and descend slabs to the E of the crest, which ends with a couple of steep, exposed moves down a sharp arête. Known as **The Imposter**, it is fine in the dry but rather loose towards the bottom where it was hit by a lightning strike in 2008. A descent 10m further left (N) is more solid and less exposed.

Summit of Clach Glas
5
The Imposter
i
ii
iv
Bealach Tower
iii
v
The Putting Green

South Ridge, Clach Glas (Mod)

i Carry on S along the horizontal ridge from the base of The Imposter, ignoring a gully on the right after 70m. Continue on the ridge and descend slabs to the left and you'll reach a ledge and path.

ii Follow a scree path then broken rocks back right down slabs and loose rock.

iii Head back left towards the Loch Slapin side down a ramp of slabs and corners, which leads into a short chimney. Descend a sloping terrace to a gap with gullies on both sides. Scramble into the gap and exit more easily. Another gap is harder to exit.

iv When you reach the crest of **Bealach Tower**, head left to cross the ridge by a small cleft. A slab heads down to a distinctive brown cone sheet. This leads right to a gap with a boulder wedged in it. Exit the gap by the right side and follow the ridge to a grassy oasis known as **The Putting Green** (possible escape route down into Choire a'Caise but it's a hard scree descent lower down).

v NE face of Bla Bheinn (Difficult). Leave the Putting Green by a path that first curves left then back right to a gap after about 100m. This is the crux of the whole route, especially if it is wet.

vi Climb out by the steep 5m wall opposite either to the left, right or middle. They are all graded Difficult and can be quite tricky in the wet. There's a perfectly shaped rock at the top for direct belay or a sling.

It is possible to escape down the screes below this wall to Choire a' Caise if it proves too wet or hard. Another alternative is to descend a gully right of the wall for 13m then ascend either a gully filled with blocks or a groove to reach the terrace further on from the top of the 5m wall.

Bla Bheinn

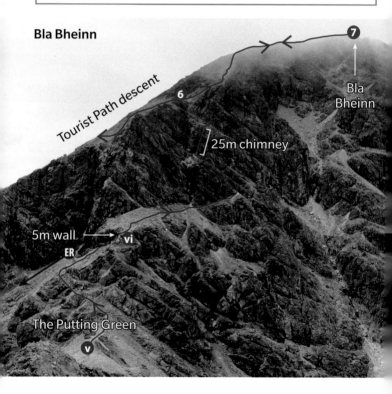

Composite photo of climber descending the Imposter

Go up the screes above then traverse further right to a stone chute about 70m W of the difficult wall. The chute leads back left up a fault/gully to a bay with the 25m Chimney (Moderate) to the right. This looks intimidating but the rock and gear placements are good and the crux is the polished start. Climb past a chockstone and move out onto the right wall.

Turn right above the chimney and then follow the gully back left to emerge on the path of the E flank route, which leads to the summit of **Bla Bheinn**.

6 Follow path to the summit (in around 15 minutes)

7 Retrace your steps down the path and continue to descend the tourist path into **Coire Uaigneich** and follow the **Allt na Dunaiche** back to the car.

Bidein

Bealach Harta

3

7

An Caisteal

8

9

10 A

11

Sgurr na Bhairnich

6

5

4

S buttress, E face of An Caisteal (Dif)

Route 10
Central South Buttress, An Caisteal

Start	Park at the Fairy Pools
Grade	Difficult
Time	8–9hr
Altitude	Up to 958m (3145ft)
Aspect	Faces SE
Conditions	Given the remote nature and length of the route, it is best in good conditions, especially the initial entry pitch and slabs.

This is potentially the most adventurous practice route in the book. A remote location, a long walk in, a big rock face with tricky route finding all mean this route is not to be underestimated. It's another route that is not of particular traverse relevance but it does enable you to check out the section from An Caisteal to Bruach na Frithe.

1 Cross the road and follow the path then Allt Coir' a' Tairneilear into **Coir' a' Tairneilear**.

2 Ascend scree to **Bealach Harta**.

3 Descend scree and rocks below Bealach Harta then contour round to below the E face of An Caisteal. Allow about 2hr 30min hours for the approach.

4 S Buttress (Difficult, 400m). The crux is the initial steep band of rock. Scramble up the gully dividing the central and S buttresses until your progress is barred by a large overhang.

5 Climb up to gain a downward sloping ledge on the left of the gully. Descend this slabby ledge, which is narrow, and can be damp and dirty with loose rocks and has a low roof above it. One climber described it as 'a very three-dimensional pitch'. This leads to a square ledge and possible belay.

6 From the ledge, climb up onto the slabs above. Zigzag to find the easiest line, traversing to bypass overlaps. Aim left towards the crest of the buttress rather than being lured back towards the steep drops into South Gully. As height is gained, the buttress narrows and easy scrambling leads to a narrow arête.

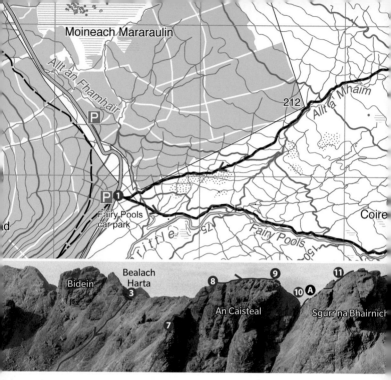

7 The arête has a massive drop to the left and a gully to the right. Follow the arête, taking care with loose rock. Head up a wide, slabby gully for a few metres before cutting right to gain the crest of the buttress to its right. Continue right to cross the head of a gully before ascending a short chimney and reaching the S ridge of An Caisteal.

8 S ridge, An Caisteal (2). Follow the ridge to the summit. Several gaps are crossed, the last one being the most spectacular. The bold will jump or stride across but the prudent will descend a slab to the right.

9 N ridge, An Caisteal (3 plus abseil or Moderate down-climb). Do not proceed beyond the summit or you will end up at the infamous 'Belly Crawl' abseil point. Retrace your steps S to and turn sharply NW and cross the ridge to the Glen Brittle side. Descend fairly steeply and contour round to a levelling off with distinctive brown screes off to the right.

Descend the narrow and exposed N ridge to a deep gully, which bars further progress (or descend slabs and short walls E of the crest).

⑩ Most people abseil from the slings but the down-climb is nowhere near as hard as it looks and the crux is right at the end just above the ground. Climb down a steep corner going left to start then cutting back right before making a couple of steep moves down into the gully.

⑪ Traverse of Sgurr na Bairnich (2). Leave the gully at the foot of the abseil and head left (W) up loose scree/path. Veer back right to the ridge and continue to an orange dyke cutting across the ridge. Ahead is a steep wall that can be taken direct (Difficult), but it is usually skirted to the right.

Continue to the summit of Sgurr na Bairnich then descend to the start of Bruach na Frithe's S ridge.

⑫ S ridge, Bruach na Frithe (2). This involves mainly walking along a rocky ridge with a few short scrambles. The last real difficulty is crossing a small gap that is entered from the left side of the ridge. Go behind a large, obvious large rock and traverse a slab rightwards. Continue more easily to the summit of Bruach na Frithe and the only trig point on the ridge.

⑬ NW ridge, Bruach na Frithe (2). This is another ridge with fine views to both sides. For a more interesting descent, seek out a more direct line on the crest but difficulties can be bypassed by scree and faint paths to the left. The ridge leads down to **Bealach a' Mhaim**.

⑭ Follow the path back to the **Fairy Pools** and return to the Fairy Pools car park.

High on An Caisteal where a narrow arête with large drops on either side has to be crossed

The Cuillin traverse in winter

The Cuillin traverse in winter

2018's fantastic conditions led to a huge upsurge in interest in the traverse of the ridge in winter and probably more people achieved this highly sought after goal that year than in the whole of the previous decade. Success was due to a number of factors, primarily a fantastic winter (with people doing the ridge from early January right through March) combined with the dissemination of information via social media.

Uisdean Hawthorn set a stunning new record of 4 hours and 57 minutes. However, you don't need to be a honed athlete or even a youngster to enjoy the best Alpinesque ridge in the UK; I was 54 and did it twice in two weeks. Admittedly, I know the ridge well and waited for perfect conditions but the ridge is probably achievable by many suitably experienced people in winter conditions.

The In Pinn in full winter glory with a climber to put the scene into perspective

Keys to success

Knowledge

A good knowledge of the ridge will help a lot but it needs to be winter-specific since summer traverses generally go in the opposite direction. Winter is best done north to south, thus enabling lots of major technicalities to be abseiled rather than climbed.

Fitness

The fitter you are, the better since it is going to be a long day/s for most people. Your fitness needs to be

hill-related. It won't hurt to be able to climb mega hard winter routes but it's not a prerequisite. More important is the ability to keep going all day, to be happy soloing across steep and serious terrain relatively quickly. As with the summer traverse, it's also a mental issue; speed balanced against safety. The terrain is never too hard yet there is the constant exposure, the need to stay totally switched on for kilometre after kilometre.

Conditions

Many people speak of suffering on the ridge, having gone for it in sub-optimal conditions. Too much snow and it will be a slog at best, impossible at worst. Too little and it might be crampons on/off ad nauseum.

Styrofoam *névé* (snow) makes for perfect placements and rapid traverses but ideal conditions aren't just about the snow and ice. It's a huge help if the ridge is tracked out which simplifies navigation (but do remain switched on and don't just blindly follow footsteps regardless), saves energy and reduces the perceived seriousness of the undertaking.

It's also useful to know if all the abseil tat is in place, not just for speed and ease but because it saves time faffing around uncovering anchors.

Weather

It goes without saying that your chances of success completing a winter traverse increase exponentially with good, clear conditions and low winds. Not only is navigation easier, the views are a fantastic morale booster and you are not constantly battling spindrift, being battered by winds.

Strategy

Even in 2010, seasoned guides were talking about allowing three days but now the majority of traverses are done in a day. My first traverse combined the best of both strategies. We went light and fast-ish (for us old codgers) but had pre-placed bivi gear in Coire Lagan. We arrived at Sgurr Alasdair with two hours of daylight so we could have finished but instead descended the Great Stone Chute to bivi. We had a great night's sleep and an easy second day. The two-day style meant we could take it easy with plenty of time for filming and photography but it was only enjoyable because of the pre-placed bivi gear. Had we been carrying full bivi gear, the enjoyment factor would have been seriously reduced and the vicious circle of extra weight causing slower progress would have been implemented.

My second traverse was light and fast-ish. We were a group of three, which was nice and sociable, meant less shared gear for each to carry and provided added security if anything went wrong. It was a better experience doing it in one day, and would be my recommendation. It was a huge day for us, being awake for about 21 hours.

Gear

Presumably if you are serious about the winter traverse, you'll be an experienced winter climber, so there are just a few basic points to note:

- Take two ice tools each and crampons and associated winter gear – the lighter the better. Nothing too technical is necessary, light and comfortable being the most important criteria.
- Light and comfortable should also apply to your boot choice. Make sure you are used to wearing them for very long days.
- Most people's rope choice will be governed by what they already own. We took a 55m half rope. The length had pros and cons; it was beneficial for some of the abseils and helped reduced down-climbing. However, 50m would have worked fine and meant less to coil/uncoil and carry. A single, pretty skinny rope of 50m would be ideal.
- A small rack will hopefully reflects your confidence and competence. We took:
  - Nuts 3,4,6,8 on a wiregate
  - The three smallest Rockcentrics each on an individual wiregate
  - 3 x 120cm slings on screwgates
  - 2 x 60cm sling on two wiregates each
  - 1 extra screwgate
  - 2 extra wiregates
  - Abseil tat to back up anchors or for emergency uses
- You'll need a personal harness, helmet, belay device and prussic loops.
- We carried a litre of water each on the second traverse and were able to supplement this by adding snow to the diminishing water and letting it melt. The real morale booster was taking a small stove for a hot brew at

Climber heading up slabs from third top of Sgurr a' Mhadaidh to the main summit

the In Pinn and a good safeguard if we were stuck out for the night.

- We had a bothy bag between us and a duvet jacket each.
- Take lightweight waterproofs; if you need heavyweight shells then perhaps conditions probably aren't right. It's easy to bail out from most of the ridge and descend to Glen Brittle quickly if things change so go light and be prepared to quit if necessary.

Approaches

Sgurr nan Gillean is the start of the ridge and has a variety of possible approaches:

- The W ridge is probably the quickest and most direct with the big advantage of being able to leave your pack either at Bealach a Bhastier or the top of the abseil chimney.
- The SE ridge is more straightforward but a bit longer approach and you have to hump your pack up and over the summit.
- Pinnacle Ridge is the classy approach but going to be more time-consuming.

Refer to the topo booklet for detailed descriptions of each approach, but note that route descriptions will need to be reversed.

Route 11

The winter traverse

Start	Sgurr nan Gillean
Grade	IV, 6
Conditions	The grade can vary enormously depending on conditions and how banked out, or not, things are. Typically, the E ridge of the In Pinn can vary from dry, snow-free rock to scary IV, 4 in full winter conditions. The exit from the T-D Gap via its short side will always be the crux with a technical grade of 6. Well 'ard climbers may manage this, cowboys may be able to lasso the top, but the majority opt to descend into Coir' a' Ghrunnda. A good snow covering will be a prerequisite for success, but it needs to be of the right sort. High-quality névé along the crest is ideal.

It is assumed anyone attempting the winter traverse will have a wealth of experience and ideally summer knowledge of the ridge. The route description is thus a lot less detailed than the one for summer. Conditions in winter vary enormously and there will be many judgement calls to be made. Note that the escape routes marked on these winter maps can also be used in summer

Sgurr nan Gillean to Bealach nan Lice

❶ Summit of **Sgurr nan Gillean**. Descend the W ridge and abseil down chimney from large block although sometimes this is banked out and if used a bit might well be stepped out making an abseil unnecessary. Continue down to Bealach a' Bhasteir.

❷ From Bealach a' Bhasteir head up **Am Basteir**. It looks very intimidating but is actually very straightforward with the Bad Step (which is often a problem in summer for less confident climbers) often being banked out to the extent of hardly being noticeable.

❸ From the summit of Am Basteir, descend to a rift W of the summit and abseil in the direction of Lota Coire. The longer your rope the better since it is followed by down-climbing slabs to the Bhasteir Nick. Ascend the **Bhasteir Tooth** then return to the Nick and squeeze through a small cave at the top of King's Cave Chimney.

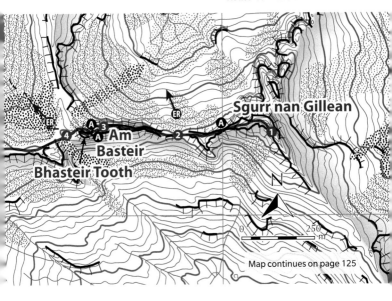

Map continues on page 125

If it's blocked by snow or ice, it's often possible to down-climb (on the left (W) as you face towards Sgurr a' Bhasteir) in a very exposed position to reach the front of the cave. The abseil is long and steep and requires a 50m rope doubled in summer but often banked out a lot in winter. From the base of the abseil, head up to Bealach nan Lice.

Bealach nan Lice to Bealach Harta

❹ From Bealach nan Lice, it's a straightforward ascent to Bruach na Frithe. In flat light/poor visibility, this featureless terrain can be surprisingly difficult to navigate.

❺ Descend the S ridge, which can often have huge cornices and stunning views across to much of the ridge ahead. Continue up the ridge to the summit of **Sgurr na Bhairnich**.

❻ Traverse down and contour round on the Glen Brittle side to the gap before An Caisteal.

❼ Climb steeply up the line of summer abseil/down-climb. Go up slightly (or not, if it's banked out with snow), traverse right, then back left up a series of corners. It

can vary from a simple solo to 1m deep powder snow flounder. **An Caisteal** is very exposed with steep drops either side and several gaps to cross.

Descend to Bealach Harta either by the summer line of heading left then back right along a ramp line, or take a more direct line.

Bealach Harta to Bealach na Glaic Moire

❽ From **Bealach Harta**, zigzag up the N top of Bidean. Abseil from an awkward, low spike directly above the steep gully that blocks access to the central peak (rather than the line of the summer route, which is to the right on the Glen Brittle side).

From the base of the abseil, ignore the slabs/corners of the abseil/down-climb in summer and traverse out further left to bypass difficulties and head back right to the slabs of the main summit. It obviously depends on the conditions, but the slabs can vary from a thin glaze of ice to a romp up perfect névé. Use your nose for the best line, which is usually via snowed-up slabs on the Harta Coire side with steep more icy steps linking them on the S side of the face.

❾ From **Bidein's main summit** (869m), descend via an obvious dyke, which is fairly easy to down-climb but steepens lower down, and there is a useful block to abseil down to the Bridge Rock in the gap before the western top. Climb up slabs from Bridge Rock and continue past the W top and descend to Bealach na Glaic Moire.

Bidein can be bypassed on the Glen Brittle side along snow/scree between Bealach Harta and Bealach na Glaic Moire.

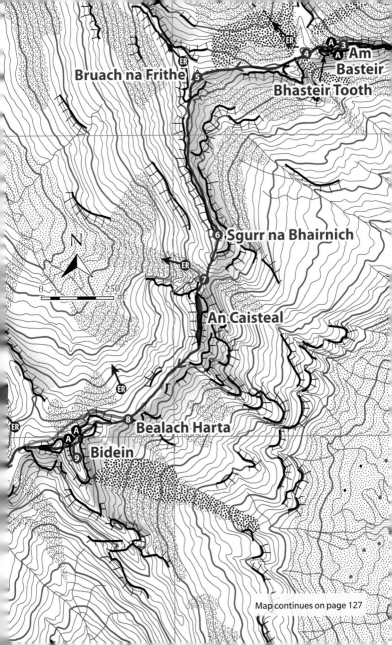

Bruach na Frithe

Am Basteir

Bhasteir Tooth

Sgurr na Bhairnich

An Caisteal

Bealach Harta

Bidein

Map continues on page 127

Winter (Bidein and Sgurr a' Mheadaidh)

Sgurr Mhic Choinnich

Sgurr Alasdair

Inaccessible Pinnacle

Bidein main summit

9

A

W top

N top

First top Sgurr a' Mheadaidh

Second top

11

Sgurr a' Ghreadaidh

Sgurr na Banachdich

Bealach na Glaic Moire

10

Bealach Harta

8

Map continues on page 129

Bealach na Glaic Moire to An Dorus

10 **Leave Bealach na Glaic Moire** and make a long slog up to the first top of Sgurr a' Mhadaidh. The four tops of Sgurr a' Mhadaidh are one of the most complicated sections and previous summer knowledge will be a definite advantage.

The first top is straightforward. A small gap separates the first and second tops. Continue until a steep rockface bars further progress

11 Abseil steeply from the second top for about 20m. The third top is more compli-cated. Ignore an easier looking gully and continue towards the end of the summit to an easy descent of a windy gully towards the W end of the S face for about 50m to an abseil from a spike and nut placement. The abseil is about 15m to descend a steep cliff.

Follow the ridge up slabby ground and cross a deep gully on the left, which is often banked out with snow, and follow the ridge to the main summit of Sgurr a' Mhadaidh.

12 Descend short steps and snow slopes to **An Dorus**, a steep-sided gap and notional midpoint of the ridge, which can be so banked out as to be hardly noticeable.

The four tops of Sgurr a' Mhadaidh

Sgurr nan Gillean

Am Basteir

Bruch na Frithe

First top

Second top

Third top

11

A

A

Sgurr a' Mhadaidh main top (918m)

12

13

An Dorus

Eag Dubh

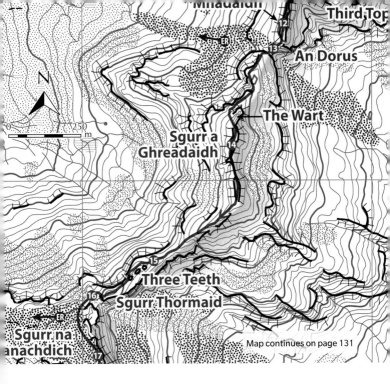

Map continues on page 131

An Dorus to Sgurr Dearg

13 Continue up snow slopes/slabs, passing the steep-sided chimney of Eag Dubh and the rocky buttress known as The Wart to reach the summit of **Sgurr a' Ghreadaidh**.

14 Descend Sgurr a' Ghreadaidh's S ridge. This is an awesome part of the Cuillin Ridge but, if conditions allow, it is possible to speedily bypass much of it by traversing snow slopes below the ridge on the Glen Brittle side.

15 Depending on the amount of snow, **The Three Teeth** can be bypassed to the left or right or straight over the top. The right-hand bypass is usually the easier option.

Snow slopes/slabs lead up to **Sgurr Thormaid** with a steep descent to the bealach between it and Sgurr na Banachdich.

16 Leave the bealach and head up **Sgurr na Banachdich**.

17 For the descent, either stick to the ridge or, if snow conditions allow, bypass the central and S tops by traversing slopes on the Glen Brittle side. Continue down to Bealach Coire na Banachdich.

18 From **Bealach Coire na Banachdich**, work your way up the slopes of Sgurr Dearg to the summit ridge which overlooks the In Pinn.

Sgurr Dearg to Bealach Coire Lagan

19 Descend slabs to the **In Pinn**. Conditions on the In Pinn will vary enormously from rimed up rock to deep snow to clear rock. Most parties traverse under it then turn back to do the traditional E ridge, which usually gets a grade of IV(4). In the right conditions, it can be a pleasure on bare rock in alpine surroundings but often it will be covered in treacherous depths of snow. Deep snow will make the W ridge all but impossible unless your cowboy skills enable the flake at 10m to be lassoed.
The abseil from the in situ chain/maillon is about 17m.

20 **An Stac** is usually bypassed via slabs on the Coire Lagan side. This can be easy and fast if the slabs are iced/snowed up, and it leads to Bealach Coire Lagan.

Climbers descending the An Stac bypass

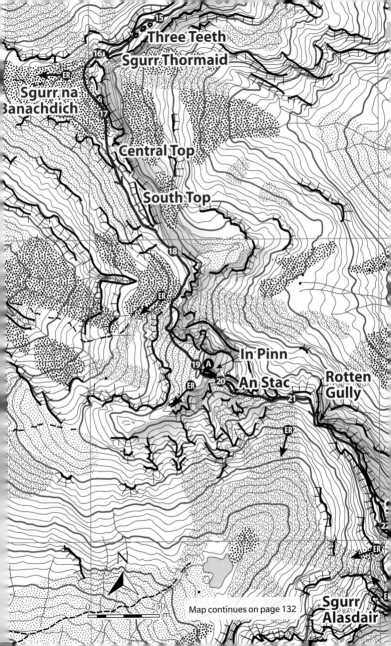

Three Teeth

Sgurr Thormaid

Sgurr na
Banachdich

Central Top

South Top

In Pinn

An Stac

Rotten
Gully

Sgurr
Alasdair

Map continues on page 132

N

0 _ _ _ _ 250
m

Bealach Coire Lagan to Sgurr Thearlaich

21 From Bealach Coire Lagan, the ascent of Sgurr Mhic Choinnich is fairly obvious. Avoid the deeply incut head of Rotten Gully then trend up and left to reach
the main crest. Easy but exposed, the ridge leads to a chimney (which can be
descended to reach Collie's Ledge. This is a useful bypass instead of abseiling
King's Chimney).

Continue up the slabby ridge to the summit.

22 From the summit of **Sgurr Mhic Choinnich**, the most direct descent is to abseil
King's Chimney. The alternative is to retrace your steps and descend to Collie's
Ledge.

King's Chimney, despite being a large feature, can be surprisingly hard
to locate in poor visibility; descend crest from summit cairn eastwards then

down and left for about 50m. A large block at the top of the chimney provides the anchor and a 50m rope will get you to the ledges that lead down to Collie's Ledge – but a longer rope obviously gives more leeway. It can be a bit awkward descending to Collie's then to the bealach but various chockstones/flakes offer another shorter abseil if necessary.

㉓ Leave Bealach Mhic Choinnich. Here, summer knowledge, especially of the Coruisk side bypass, will be useful.

The bypass on the Coruisk side is the most straightforward but it can be banked out and a fairly exposed position. Given the right snow conditions, it can be fairly easy to climb snowed-up slabs and follow the ridge.

Sgurr Thearlaich via Sgurr Alasdair to T-D Gap

The descent from the summit of **Sgurr Thearlaich** is fairly steep and there may well be in situ abseil tat. Scramble down the ridge towards the T-D Gap then cut back right to top of Great Stone Chute (or abseil down fairly directly to Chute).

㉔ From the top of the Great Chute, **Sgurr Alasdair** is accessed by its SE ridge, which is an easy ascent and descent. After returning to the top of the Great Stone Chute, descend to the very obvious barrier of the **T-D Gap**.

T-D Gap to Caisteal a' Garbh-choire

㉕ It's a 20m abseil from in situ slings at the top of the T-D Gap. The climb out of the gap opposite the abseil is the crux of the ridge but most parties avoid it. Unless massively banked out, it will have a technical grade of 6. Again, the cowboys may be able to lasso the spike at the top for aid but most parties exit the gap on the **Coir' a' Ghrunnda** side by either down-climbing or abseiling. There are often abseil slings on the choke of boulders at the foot of the abseil. Given good snow conditions, the down-climb can be easy but beware the steepening right at the base of the gully. Contour round to Bealach Coir' an Lochain.

㉖ Ascend **Sgurr Dubh an Da Bheinn.**

㉗ From the summit, you can decide whether or not to go out to Sgurr Dubh Mor, a Munro but not actually on the ridge. It's an optional Munro tick, which most parties bypass but it's well worth the effort.

㉘ From **Sgurr Dubh Mor**, retrace your steps to Sgurr Dubh an Da Bheinn or consider the direct line (this goes from the col below the SW spur of Sgurr Dubh Mor and basically contours around below the main cliffs to Caisteal a' Garbh-choire). Once you're back at Sgurr Dubh an Da Bheinn, descend to Caisteal a' Garbh-choire.

View from Sgurr Dubh an Da Bheinn towards Gars-bheinn and the end of the ridge

Gars-bheinn

Sgurr a' Choire Bhig

F

Sgurr nan Eag

31

30

Caisteal' Garbh-choire

29

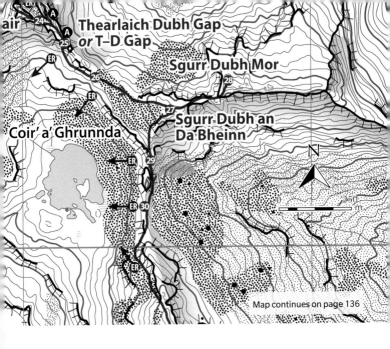

Map continues on page 136

29 Skirt Caisteal a' Garbh-choire on the Coruisk side.

The rest of the ridge out to Gars-bheinn is technically easy but a long slog. Gird your loins and just do it rather than taking the easy way out and descending to Glen Brittle via Coir' a' Ghrunnda. One option if the weather is good is to dump everything and just take a single axe each and head out to the end of the ridge then return and descend with packs into Ghrunnda. This is a sound choice if conditions are skinny with lots of bare rock because the scree descent from Gars-bheinn won't be pleasant unless it's snowed over. It's a much more pleasant descent into Coir' a' Ghrunnda and down to the path back to Glen Brittle.

Caisteal a' Garbh-choire to Gars-bheinn

30 From Bealach a' Garbh-choire, the easiest line of ascent up Sgurr nan Eag is up the rocks and scree on the Glen Brittle side of the ridge line but for more interest this can be taken in a more direct line.

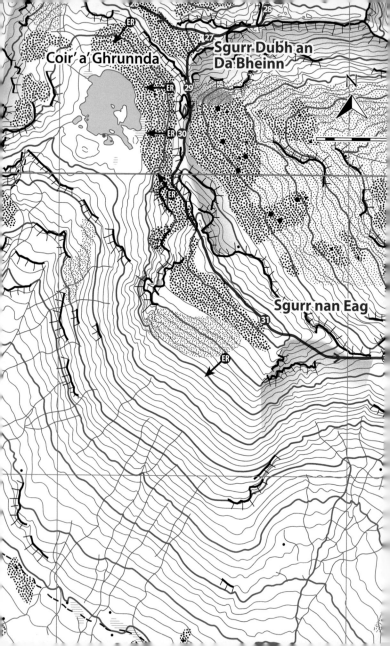

Coir' a' Ghrunnda

Sgurr Dubh an
Da Bheinn

Sgurr nan Eag

31 From the summit of **Sgurr nan Eag**, the last Munro, stay switched on. Keep your wits about you especially in less than optimum visibility as it's all too easy to make navigational errors here. Make sure to get the right line down to Sgurr a' Choir Bhig and do not be lured off the end of Sgurr nan Eag by the spur going SSW instead of the SE.

32 In good snow conditions there is no need to stay on the ridge to the summit of **Sgurr a' Choir Bhig**. It can often be quicker and easier quicker to contour round on snow slopes on the Glen Brittle side. Continue to **Gars-bheinn**. You've reached the end. Descend SW to the path back to Glen Brittle or return via Coir' a' Ghrunnda.

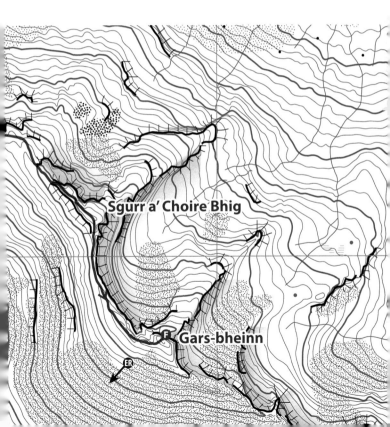

Appendix A
Summary of classic scrambles

Route number	Route name	Grade	Time
1	Round of Fionn Choire	1/2	5–6hr
2	The Spur, Sgurr an Fheadain	2	4–5hr
3	South South East Buttress, Sgurr na Stri	2/3	4–5hr
4	Thuilm Ridge, Sgurr a' Mhadaidh	3/Moderate	5–6hr
5	South Ridge, Sgurr Coir' an Lochain	Difficult	6–7hr
6	The Dubh Ridge	Moderate	7hr 30min–8hr 30min
7	Round of Coire Lagan	Difficult	10hr
8	Pinnacle Ridge, Sgurr nan Gillean	3	6hr 30min–7hr 30min
9	Clach Glas – Bla Bheinn Traverse	Difficult	6hr 30 min–7hr 30min
10	Central South Buttress, An Caisteal	Difficult	8–9hr

Appendix B
Further reading, webcams and accommodation

Further reading

Noel Williams, *Skye Scrambles* (Scottish Mountaineering Club, 2011)

Mike Lates, *Skye: The Cuillin* (Scottish Mountaineering Club, 2011).
> Both these SMC books have a lot of information and good detailed descriptions of the ridge. If Cuillin obsession was a religion, then these can be seen as the Old and New Testaments.

Tom Prentice, *The Cuillin & Other Skye Mountains* (Mica Publishing, 2019).
> This book provides encyclopedic coverage of not just the Cuillin but also other Skye hills.

Gordon Stainforth, *The Cuillin: The Great Mountain Ridge of Skye* (Constable, 2002).
> A visual extravaganza, long out of print but available (at great expense) on Abe Books or Amazon, this is still the definitive coffee table book about the Cuillin. Try to beg, borrow or steal a copy.

Andy Hyslop, *Skye Ridge* (Rockfax, 2002).
> www.rockfax.com/climbing-guides/miniguides/skye-ridge/ Although perhaps a bit scant and geared towards running the ridge, it is still a useful download. This is in the process of being updated.

The website and Facebook group All Things Cuillin (run by the author) contain lots of info and photos and regular updates on weather and conditions; https://allthingscuillin.co.uk/, www.facebook.com/groups/165143940728168/.

Webcams

www.camvista.com/scotland/highlands/skye.php3
(from the Skye bridge looking towards the Cuillin)

www.baysider.com/Webcams/United_Kingdom/Sligachan/Sligachan_Hotel/
(Looking at the northern Cuillin from Sligachan)

Accommodation

Sligachan campsite – www.sligachan.co.uk/camping/

Glen Brittle campsite – www.dunvegancastle.com/glenbrittle/campsite/

Camasunary Bothy – www.mountainbothies.org.uk

Glen Brittle Youth Hostel – www.hostellingscotland.org.uk/hostels/glenbrittle

Broadford Youth Hostel – www.hostellingscotland.org.uk/hostels/broadford

Glen Brittle Memorial Hut – www.gbmh.co.uk

Coruisk (JMCS) Hut – www.glasgowjmcs.org.uk/coruisk.php

Listing of Cicerone guides

SCOTLAND

Backpacker's Britain:
Northern Scotland
Ben Nevis and Glen Coe
Cycle Touring in Northern Scotland
Cycling in the Hebrides
Great Mountain Days in Scotland
Mountain Biking in Southern and
Central Scotland
Mountain Biking in West and North
West Scotland
Not the West Highland Way
Scotland
Scotland's Best Small Mountains
Scotland's Mountain Ridges
The Ayrshire and Arran Coastal
Paths
The Border Country
The Borders Abbeys Way
The Cape Wrath Trail
The Great Glen Way
The Great Glen Way Map Booklet
The Hebridean Way
The Hebrides
The Isle of Mull
The Isle of Skye
The Skye Trail
The Southern Upland Way
The Speyside Way
The Speyside Way Map Booklet
The West Highland Way
Walking Highland Perthshire
Walking in Scotland's Far North
Walking in the Angus Glens
Walking in the Cairngorms
Walking in the Ochils, Campsie Fells
and Lomond Hills
Walking in the Pentland Hills
Walking in the Southern Uplands
Walking in Torridon
Walking Loch Lomond and
the Trossachs
Walking on Arran
Walking on Harris and Lewis
Walking on Jura, Islay and Colonsay
Walking on Rum and the Small Isles
Walking on the Orkney and
Shetland Isles
Walking on Uist and Barra
Walking the Corbetts
Vol 1 South of the Great Glen
Walking the Corbetts
Vol 2 North of the Great Glen

Walking the Galloway Hills
Walking the Munros Vol 1 –
Southern, Central and Western
Highlands
Walking the Munros Vol 2 –
Northern Highlands and the
Cairngorms
West Highland Way Map Booklet
Winter Climbs Ben Nevis and
Glen Coe
Winter Climbs in the Cairngorms

NORTHERN ENGLAND TRAILS

Hadrian's Wall Path
Hadrian's Wall Path Map Booklet
Pennine Way Map Booklet
The Coast to Coast Map Booklet
The Coast to Coast Walk
The Dales Way
The Dales Way Map Booklet
The Pennine Way

LAKE DISTRICT

Cycling in the Lake District
Great Mountain Days in the
Lake District
Lake District Winter Climbs
Lake District:
High Level and Fell Walks
Lake District:
Low Level and Lake Walks
Mountain Biking in the Lake District
Outdoor Adventures with Children
– Lake District
Scrambles in the Lake District
– North
Scrambles in the Lake District
– South
Short Walks in Lakeland
Book 2: North Lakeland
The Cumbria Way
The Southern Fells
Tour of the Lake District
Trail and Fell Running in the Lake
District
Walking the Lake District Fells
– Langdale
Walking the Lake District Fells
– Wasdale

NORTH WEST ENGLAND AND THE ISLE OF MAN

Cycling the Pennine Bridleway
Cycling the Way of the Roses
Isle of Man Coastal Path
The Lancashire Cycleway
The Lune Valley and Howgills
The Ribble Way
Walking in Cumbria's Eden Valley
Walking in Lancashire
Walking in the Forest of Bowland
and Pendle
Walking on the Isle of Man
Walking on the West
Pennine Moors

Walks in Ribble Country
Walks in Silverdale and Arnside

NORTH EAST ENGLAND, YORKSHIRE DALES AND PENNINES

Cycling in the Yorkshire Dales
Great Mountain Days in the
Pennines
Mountain Biking in the
Yorkshire Dales
South Pennine Walks
St Oswald's Way and St Cuthbert's
Way
The Cleveland Way and the
Yorkshire Wolds Way
The Cleveland Way Map Booklet
The North York Moors
The Reivers Way
The Teesdale Way
Trail and Fell Running in the
Yorkshire Dales
Walking in County Durham
Walking in Northumberland
Walking in the North Pennines
Walking in the Yorkshire Dales:
North and East
Walking in the Yorkshire Dales:
South and West
Walks in the Yorkshire Dales

WALES AND WELSH BORDERS

Cycle Touring in Wales
Cycling Lon Las Cymru
Glyndwr's Way
Great Mountain Days in Snowdonia
Hillwalking in Shropshire
Hillwalking in Wales – Vol 1
Hillwalking in Wales – Vol 2
Mountain Walking in Snowdonia
Offa's Dyke Map Booklet
Offa's Dyke Path
Pembrokeshire Coast Path
Map Booklet
Ridges of Snowdonia
Scrambles in Snowdonia
Snowdonia: Low-level and easy
walks – North
The Cambrian Way
The Ceredigion and Snowdonia
Coast Paths
The Pembrokeshire Coast Path
The Severn Way
The Snowdonia Way
The Wales Coast Path
The Wye Valley Walk
Walking in Carmarthenshire
Walking in Pembrokeshire
Walking in the Forest of Dean
Walking in the Wye Valley
Walking on the Brecon Beacons
Walking on the Gower
Walking the Shropshire Way

Trekking in the Dolomites
Via Ferratas of the
 Italian Dolomites Vol 1
Via Ferratas of the
 Italian Dolomites: Vol 2
Walking and Trekking in the
 Gran Paradiso
Walking in Abruzzo
Walking in Italy's Cinque Terre
Walking in Italy's Stelvio
 National Park
Walking in Sardinia
Walking in Sicily
Walking in the Dolomites
Walking in Tuscany
Walking in Umbria
Walking Lake Como and Maggiore
Walking Lake Garda and Iseo
Walking on the Amalfi Coast
Walks and Treks in the
 Maritime Alps

BELGIUM AND LUXEMBOURG
The GR5 Trail – Benelux and
 Lorraine
Walking in the Ardennes

SCANDINAVIA:
 NORWAY, SWEDEN, FINLAND
Trekking the Kungsleden
Walking in Norway

POLAND, SLOVAKIA, ROMANIA,
 HUNGARY AND BULGARIA
The Danube Cycleway Vol 2
The High Tatras
The Mountains of Romania
Walking in Bulgaria's National Parks
Walking in Hungary

SLOVENIA, CROATIA, SERBIA,
 MONTENEGRO, ALBANIA
 AND KOSOVO
Mountain Biking in Slovenia
The Islands of Croatia
The Julian Alps of Slovenia
The Mountains of Montenegro
The Peaks of the Balkans Trail
The Slovene Mountain Trail
Walking in Slovenia: The Karavanke
Walks and Treks in Croatia

SPAIN
Camino de Santiago – Camino
 Frances
Coastal Walks in Andalucia
Cycle Touring in Spain
Cycling the Camino de Santiago
Mountain Walking in Mallorca
Mountain Walking in
 Southern Catalunya
Spain's Sendero Historico: The GR1
The Andalucian Coast to Coast Walk
The Camino del Norte and
 Camino Primitivo
The Camino Ingles and Ruta do Mar

The Mountains of Nerja
The Mountains of Ronda
 and Grazalema
The Northern Caminos
The Sierras of Extremadura
Trekking in Mallorca
Trekking in the Canary Islands
Walking and Trekking in the
 Sierra Nevada
Walking in Andalucia
Walking in Menorca
Walking in the Cordillera Cantabrica
Walking on Gran Canaria
Walking on La Gomera and El Hierro
Walking on La Palma
Walking on Lanzarote and
 Fuerteventura
Walking on Tenerife
Walking on the Costa Blanca
Walking the Camino dos Faros

PORTUGAL
Portugal's Rota Vicentina
The Camino Portugues
Walking in Portugal
Walking in the Algarve
Walking on Madeira
Walking on the Azores

GREECE
The High Mountains of Crete
Trekking in Greece
Walking and Trekking in Zagori
Walking and Trekking on Corfu

CYPRUS
Walking in Cyprus

MALTA
Walking on Malta

INTERNATIONAL CHALLENGES,
 COLLECTIONS AND ACTIVITIES
Canyoning in the Alps
Europe's High Points
The Via Francigena
 Canterbury to Rome – Part 2

MOROCCO
Mountaineering in the Moroccan
 High Atlas
The High Atlas
Walks and Scrambles in the
 Moroccan Anti-Atlas

TANZANIA
Kilimanjaro

SOUTH AFRICA
Walking in the Drakensberg

TAJIKISTAN
Trekking in Tajikistan

JAPAN
Hiking and Trekking in the Japan
 Alps and Mount Fuji
Japan's Kumano Kodo Pilgrimage

JORDAN
Jordan – Walks, Treks, Caves,
 Climbs and Canyons
Treks and Climbs in Wadi Rum,
 Jordan

NEPAL
Annapurna
Everest: A Trekker's Guide
Trekking in the Himalaya

BHUTAN
Trekking in Bhutan

INDIA
Trekking in Ladakh

CHINA
The Mount Kailash Trek

NORTH AMERICA:
 USA AND CANADA
The John Muir Trail
The Pacific Crest Trail

SOUTH AMERICA:
 ARGENTINA, CHILE AND PERU
Aconcagua and the Southern Andes
Hiking and Biking Peru's Inca Trails
Torres del Paine

TECHNIQUES
Fastpacking
Geocaching in the UK
Lightweight Camping
Map and Compass
Outdoor Photography
Polar Exploration
Rock Climbing
Sport Climbing
The Mountain Hut Book

MINI GUIDES
Alpine Flowers
Avalanche!
Navigation
Pocket First Aid and Wilderness
 Medicine
Snow

MOUNTAIN LITERATURE
8000 metres
A Walk in the Clouds
Abode of the Gods
Fifty Years of Adventure
The Pennine Way – the Path,
 the People, the Journey
Unjustifiable Risk?

For full information on all our
guides, books and eBooks,
visit our website:
www.cicerone.co.uk

Explore the world with Cicerone

walking • trekking • mountaineering • climbing • mountain biking • cycling • via ferratas • scrambling • trail running • skills and techniques

For over 50 years, Cicerone have built up an outstanding collection of nearly 400 guides, inspiring all sorts of amazing experiences.

www.cicerone.co.uk – where adventures begin

- Our **website** is a treasure-trove for every outdoor adventurer. You can buy books or read inspiring articles and trip reports, get technical advice, check for updates, and view videos, photographs and mapping for routes and treks.

- **Register this book** or any other Cicerone guide in your member's library on our website and you can choose to automatically access updates and GPX files for your books, if available.

- Our **fortnightly newsletters** will update you on new publications and articles and keep you informed of other news and events. You can also follow us on Facebook, Twitter and Instagram.

We hope you have enjoyed using this guidebook. If you have any comments you would like to share, please contact us using the form on our website or via email, so that we can provide the best experience for future customers.

CICERONE

Juniper House, Murley Moss Business Village, Oxenholme Road, Kendal LA9 7RL

✉ info@cicerone.co.uk   cicerone.co.uk